I0160215

George Ellis

Memoir of a Map of the Countries

Comprehended Between the Black Sea and the Caspian...

George Ellis

Memoir of a Map of the Countries
Comprehended Between the Black Sea and the Caspian...

ISBN/EAN: 9783744757430

Printed in Europe, USA, Canada, Australia, Japan

Cover: Foto ©ninafisch / pixelio.de

More available books at **www.hansebooks.com**

M E M O I R

OF A

MAP OF THE COUNTRIES

COMPREHENDED BETWEEN THE

BLACK SEA AND THE CASPIAN;

WITH AN ACCOUNT OF THE

CAUCASIAN NATIONS,

AND

VOCABULARIES OF THEIR LANGUAGES.

L O N D O N:

PRINTED FOR J. EDWARDS, IN PALL-MALL.

M.DCC.LXXX.VIII.

P R E F A C E.

IT is hoped, that the Map now offered to the public, will be found to be much fuller and more accurate than any which has yet been publifhed : it is ftill, however, very imperfect ; and many errors will doubtlefs be difcovered in it, when the countries that it reprefents fhall have been completely and accurately furveyed.*

To fuch a map it feemed neceffary to annex a few pages of narrative, and I flatter myfelf that I fhall not be thought to have trefpaffed too much on the reader's patience. What I have offered is principally drawn from the firft volume of Mr. *Gulden-ftaedt*'s Travels—from various papers inferted in the St. Peterfburgh Journal—from Dr. *Reineggs*'s Defcription of Georgia, publifhed in a periodical work by Profeffor *Pallas*—from the materials contained in *Muller*'s Sammlung Ruffifcher Gefchichte—and from

A 2   fome

---

* The latitude of the fort of *Mofdok* has been found to be 43° 43′ 46″ North. Its longitude, according to the obfervations of Profeffor *Lowitz*, is 62° 42′ 30″ ; but, according to Mr. *Guldenftaedt* (whom I have followed) 62° 27′ 30″ Faft of Ferro. *Tiffis*, according to *Guldenftaedt*, is in 41° 43′ 40″ North latitude, and very nearly on the fame meridian with *Mofdok*, although it is generally placed above a degree farther to the eaftward. *Kiflar* has been found to be in latitude 43° 51′ North, and its longitude, though it has not been obferved, may be very nearly determined by its diftance from *Mofdok*. Many other pofitions in the map have been pretty well afcertained by the marches of the Ruffian troops fince the publication of *Zannoni*'s map, which is incomparably the beft I have yet feen. Upon the whole, I have reafon to hope that I have laid down, with tolerable accuracy, the defart of Aftrachan, the Ruffian line, the interval between that line and the high mountains, and the greater part of Georgia. The country of the Lefguis, Armenia, and the Turkifh province of Achalziché, are principally taken from Zannoni. The peninfula of Taurica, and the ifland of Phanagoria (or Taman) are, I believe, correctly delineated, being copied from a furvey made by order of Prince *Potemkin* ; but their pofition is very likely to be erroneous, becaufe the great chart of the fea of Azof, and the maps publifhed by the academy of St. Peterfburgh, differ by more than a degree in the latitude of Taganrok ; befides which, the direction of the fea of Azof is very differently reprefented. Such a difference could not be reconciled ; and, by endeavouring to do fo, I have perhaps placed the ifland of Phanagoria rather too far to the northward. As to the coaft of the Black Sea to the eaftward of Sotchuk-Kalé, it has never, that I know of, been furveyed by Europeans, nor do I think that any chart of that fea is at all to be depended on,

port to their ftaple at Tanais the Afiatic productions with which they fupplied the fouthern parts of Europe, while the articles defigned for the North were conveyed to the Ruffian town of Ladoga, on the Volkhow, from whence they were tranfported to the town of Wifby, in the ifle of Gothland. The deftructive expeditions of TAMERLANE had indeed forcibly diverted the trade of Afia from this channel to that of Smyrna and Aleppo; but although the new road is obvioufly moft convenient for the productions of Arabia, the fituation of Aftrachan appears to be better calculated for the trade of Perfia and Northern India. The recovery of this place, therefore, gave rife to many fplendid fpeculations: the project of re-eftablifhing its commerce was formed by feveral fucceeding fovereigns, was nearly perfected by *Peter* the Great, and is not yet entirely relinquifhed. *Peter*, after fecuring the navigation of the Volga, eftablifhed a line of forts extending from that river near the town of Zaritfin to the Don, and thus formed a barrier of fufficient ftrength to protect the empire againft the incurfions of the predatory nations to the fouthward; but he was foon tempted to a farther extenfion of his territories by the revolution which took place in Perfia.

HUSSEIN, King of that country, had loft his crown by an infurrection to which the oppreffions of his minifters had given rife, and which his own imbecillity had encouraged: the *Afghans* were in poffeffion of Ifpahan; *Thamas*, heir to the

2   throne,

throne, was a fugitive in his own dominions; the Turks had taken up arms in order to profit of the weaknefs of Perfia, and *Peter* was almoft compelled to follow their example. He therefore fitted out a fleet at Aftrachan to attend the motions of his army, which, following the weftern coaft of the Cafpian, took poffeffion of the towns of Derbent and Baku, marched into Ghilan, and occupied nearly the whole of that fertile province, which was afterwards affured to him by a treaty with *Thamas*. Thus he became for a while fole mafter of the Cafpian, but when, by a fecond revolution, the famous *Nadir Shach* became undifputed fovereign of Perfia, the Emprefs *Anne* was glad to purchafe fome exclufive privileges for the trade of her fubjeets by the ceffion of a conqueft which it was no longer practicable to retain. On this occafion, the Ruffian fettlements which had been made with a view to preferve the communication between Ruffia and Ghilan, were removed to Kiflar, a town which had received the inhabitants of the ancient Terki; and for the protection of thefe fettlers it became neceffary to fortify the river Terek. A new line was therefore begun, but it advanced fo flowly, that in 1763 the redoubts extended no farther than Tfchervlenova, a Cofak village about 107 Englifh miles to the weftward of the mouth of the river. In the courfe of the fame year the fort of Mofdok was built about 66 miles farther weftward, and in 1770, with a view to fecure the intermediate fpace, 850 Cofak families from the Don and Volga regiments were eftablifhed at Naur,

which

which lies about half way between the two preceeding poſts. Since that time the lines have been gradually extended ſo as to reach the ſea of Azof, and to ſecure the whole ſpace included between that ſea and the Caſpian.

By the completion of theſe lines the enemies of Ruſſia are kept at a great diſtance from the more fertile provinces of the empire, and the defence of the tributary princes of Georgia and Imeretia is greatly facilitated; but on the other hand it ſeems that the almoſt daily loſs of men from the difference of Climate and water, from the bad qualities of their food (which is in part brought from a great diſtance) and from the fatigue of conſtant exertions in repelling the attacks of an enemy equally reſolute and alert, cannot but be ſeverely felt by a country ſo imperfectly peopled as Ruſſia. But whatever may be thought of this acquiſition of territory, there can be no doubt concerning the importance of another province lately added to the Ruſſian Empire; I mean the Crimea.

This peninſula, which until theſe few years was never thoroughly explored by Europeans, was very early diſtinguiſhed by its extraordinary fertility, and by its commercial advantages. Long before the time of *Herodotus* its ſouthern coaſts were occupied by Greek ſettlers, who had founded the towns of Kherſon*, Theodoſia, Panticapeum, and ſome others, and carried

on

* It is probable that the modern towns ſituated in Taurica are not built exactly on the ſite of thoſe mentioned in antiquity, but perhaps Eupatoria (the Koſlev of the Tartars) may anſwer

on a very extenfive trade with the Scythians, and with the cities of Heraclea, Trebizonde, and Byzantium. Thefe Greeks were perhaps at firft independent, but about four centuries and a half before the birth of Chrift, they became tributary to the Scythians, and continued in fubjection until the time of *Mithridates*, whom they invited to take poffeffion of their country. *Mithridates*, already mafter of Pontus and Colchis, and in clofe alliance with the Sarmatæ, eagerly embraced an offer which promifed him fuch great refources in his defigns againft the Romans. He therefore difpatched a fleet to Kherfon, and another with an army to the Palus Mæotis, difpoffeffed *Parifades*, tyrant of the Bofphorus, drove the Scythians out of Taurica, and took poffeffion of that peninfula with its dependencies, confifting of the eaftern coaft of the Palus Mæotis from Tanais to the Cuban, together with the ifland of Phanagoria. From thefe poffeffions he is faid to have drawn an annual revenue of 20,000 minæ (about 720,000 bufhels) of corn, and two talents (about 200,000 ounces) of filver. This prince was the founder of the town of Eupatorium. Being defeated by *Pompey* in Afia Minor, he retired to the Bofphorus, where, after fome ineffectual ftruggles to retrieve his affairs, he killed himfelf in defpair.

After

---

fwer nearly to the ancient Eupatorium. Sebaftopol is at a very fmall diflance from the ancient Kherfon, the ruins of which ftill remain : Baluclava is probably the *Symbol* of the Genoefe, and Portus Symbolon of Strabo : Theodofia (lately Caffa) the Theodofia of the ancients : Sudak, Soldaia : Kertfh the ancient Bofphorus, and Jenikale Panticapeum, The beft map of this country is that of Kingfbergen, publifhed at Berlin in 1776,

[6]

After his death this country became tributary to the Romans, and continued fo till the time of *Valerian*, when we find the little fovereigns, among whom it was divided, giving a paffage to the Goths into the Roman territories.

By the removal of the feat of empire from Rome to Conftantinople, the importance of the maritime coafts of the Tauric Cherfonefe was confiderably increafed: but notwithftanding the anxiety of the Greek emperors to protect this peninfula, it was fucceffively ravaged by the Sarmatæ, by the Alani*, by the

Goths

---

* Under the name of Alani were comprehended a great variety of nations. Their inhabitants, according to *Ammianus Marcellinus*, began on the eaftern fide of the Don, from whence they extended over the vaft defarts of Scythia as far as the Ganges. Thofe whofe perfons he has defcribed (proceri autem Alani pæne omnes funt, et pulchri, crinibus mediocriter flavis) were probably fome of the Tanaitæ, and of that race which we call *Fins*; becaufe yellow hair, which is fo common in the weft, is I believe in the eaftern parts of Europe peculiar to the people of Finnifh origin. The Mofchi, Aorfi, and Siraci, who are placed by *Pliny* between the Palus Mæotis, and the Cafpian, feem to anfwer to the Mockfhanes, Erfanians, and Syrains; and thefe, together with the Kermikhiones (fuppofed to be Thercmiffes) and fome others, now driven far to the northward, were perhaps the people here called Alani, and known at a later period under the name of Ougres, and White Huns.

" Parte alia (fays *Marcellinus*) prope Amazonum fedes, Alani funt Orienti acclines, diffufi per populofas gentes et amplas, Afiaticos vergentes in tractus, quos dilatari ad ufque Gangen accepi fluvium." Thefe therefore were a Caucafian nation, the fame with the Albani, and had migrated to the caftward. The only people I believe who can anfwer this defcription are the Agvhans, or Affgans, who pretend that their founder removed from the mountains of Armenia to thofe of Candahar. Colonel *Gaerber* takes it for granted that the Affghans, whom he found near Derbent, were defcendants of the Albani; and Dr. *Reineggs* contends, that the names of the two people are in fact the fame. The Armenians (fays he) cannot pronounce the letter L in the middle of a word, but call the Albans Agvhans, as they call Kalaki, Kaghaki, &c.

The

Goths (who made a permanent establishment in the mountains to the southward) by the Huns, and by the Khazari··

It is not easy to determine the precise epocha at which the Genoese established themselves in this country, but it appears to have been towards the end of the eleventh century. Their first conquest was the town of Caffa, which was taken from them by the Venetians in 1297, but soon afterwards recovered. These commercial adventurers were treated with great lenity, and even distinction, by the Tartar Khans of the Crimea, who left them in undisturbed possession of the seaports, and being still more caressed by the kings of Armenia, whose dominions in the thirteenth century extended as far as the Caspian, they soon got possession of the whole trade of the East. They had establishments at Trebizonde, Amastria, Caffa, Soldaia, Symbol, and Tana.

The name of Alani, however, is seldom used in the extensive sense adopted by *Marcellinus*, but is generally applied to those nations only who inhabited the northern slope of Caucasus from Mount Beth-Tau to the Caspian. *Rubruquis* says that the Alani were in his time called *Acias*, or *Akas* (now the Abkhas).

* The history of this people may be found in the Histoire des Huns, by *M. de Guignes*. Their prince is by the Byzantine writers called Khan (χχγινς) and their nobles Beys (Πεχ). They built a town, with the assistance of the Greeks, called Sar-kel (Σαρκελ) which, as we are told by the Emperor *Constantine*, signified in the Khozarian language, *White Town*. This place is now called Bielgorod, which means the same thing. (In the present Tartar language, I believe that Sara-Kaiah would signify the *yellow town*).

The Khazari were divided into a great number of tribes, and were possibly composed of several different nations, but the governing Horde were most probably Tartars, and perhaps the ancestors of the present Kerguis.

Tana. At length their own arrogance produced their deſtruction, by incenſing the Khans of the Crimea, whom the Porte had in vain laboured to prejudice againſt them. In 1474, the Tartars, with the aſſiſtance of the Turks, beſieged and took the town of Caffa, the laſt poſt of which the Genoeſe retained the ſovereignty.

Theſe Tartars had been eſtabliſhed in the Crimea above two centuries before the expulſion of the Genoeſe. They were ſubjects of *Batu Khan*, grandſon of *Zingis*, and their conqueſt was annexed to the kingdom of Caſan, till after the death of *Tamerlane* in 1400, when *Edegai Khan*, an officer of that prince, took poſſeſſion of it, and was ſucceeded at his death by *Deulet Gherai*, in whoſe family the ſovereignty continued till the year 1783, when the Crimea was occupied by a Ruſſian army under the command of Prince *Potemkin*.

The Tauric Cherſoneſe is divided into two parts by mountains which run nearly acroſs it from eaſt to weſt. The northern diviſion is flat, poor, and only ſit for paſturage. In the ſouthern parts the vallies are aſtoniſhingly productive, and the climate extremely mild, from the excluſion of thoſe violent winds by which the northern diviſion is frequently incommoded. The lower hills extending from Theodoſia to the eaſtern extremity of the country are principally employed in gardening, and produce excellent fruit in great abundance. Beſides the ports of

Kertſh

Kertſh and Jenikalé, the road of Caffa, and the harbour of Balu-clava, there is near Sebaſtopol one of the fineſt harbours in the world, ſecured from all winds, ſufficiently capacious to admit large fleets, and capable of receiving ſhips of any burthen. It is ſaid that the Tartar inhabitants do not at preſent exceed ſeventy thouſand. Many muſt have periſhed in their civil diſſentions, ſome in the defence of their country againſt the Ruſſians, and many more have migrated from that principle of diſlike which is generally conceived againſt a new government. But under all its preſent diſadvantages the poſſeſſion of this country ſeems to have decided for ever the conteſt for ſuperiority between the rival courts of St. Peterſburgh and Conſtantinople.

On the oppoſite ſide of the Boſphorus lies the ſmall and beautiful iſland of Phanagoria, and at a ſmall diſtance to the eaſt-ward begin the mountains of Caucaſus, which extend from hence quite to the Caſpian. From the ſouthern ſide of theſe mountains advance ſeveral lower ridges, formerly known by the name of Montes Moſchici, Pariedri, &c. on the northern ſide they throw out only a ſingle chain, called Beſh-tau (i. e. the five mountains) on which are bred thoſe beautiful Circaſſian horſes, ſo much eſteemed by the Turks, and conſidered as nearly equal to the fineſt breeds of Arabia. This ridge probably anſwers to the Montes Hippici of *Ptolemy.*

According to *Strabo,* the country extending from Phanagoria

C   to to Colchis was inhabited by the following nations. Firſt, the Sindi, cloſe to Phanagoria ; then, along the ſea ſhore, the Achæi, Zygi, and Heniochi, which extended as far as Dioſcurias (now Iſgaour) and behind them the Cercetæ and Macropogones. Of the two latter nations nothing is known, and of the three former, little more than that they were pirates, and that they ſupplied the Greeks of the Boſphorus with the ſlaves which they made in their predatory expeditions. Behind Dioſcurias, in the higheſt mountains, lived the Soanes, or Suani*, perhaps the anceſtors of the people who ſtill occupy the ſame country and retain the ſame name. They were then a formidable and numerous nation, governed by a king, with a national council of three hundred perſons. They are ſaid to have collected a conſiderable quantity of gold by means of fleeces which they ſunk in their torrents, a practice from which *Strabo* derives the Fable of the Golden Fleece. It is reported that this mode of collecting gold ſtill ſubſiſted when the Turks were in poſſeſſion of Mingrelia, and that the produce of the Zgenis-ſkalé (horſe-river, the Hippus) was farmed at Conſtantinople to certain Jews.

AT Dioſcurias began the country of Colchis, which extended nearly as far as Trebizonde. Its ſoil was fertile, its fruit delicious, and its honey excellent, though it produces ſome ſorts
which

---

* The preſent Suani are a poor and ſimple people, who ſubſiſt by raiſing cattle and by a little agriculture. They are ſubject to the prince of Imeretia. Their language appears to be a very corrupt dialect of the Georgian.

which were bitter. It furnished every article neceſſary for ſhip-building; that is to ſay, flax, hemp, wax, pitch, and wood of the beſt quality and in vaſt quantities. Its linen manufactures were much eſteemed, which was adduced as a proof that its inhabitants were of Egyptian origin. This country, after being divided into ſeveral ſmall principalities called Sceptuchiæ, fell into the hands of *Mithridates*, and after his death was again diſtributed into many diviſions.

To the eaſt of Colchis was Iberia, comprehending the preſent kingdom of Imeretia, and part of Carduel and Caket. It was well inhabited, had many villages and towns, with brick houſes regularly built, and public edifices. The Iberians of the vallies were peaceable and fond of agriculture: the mountaineers ſubſiſted by paſturage, were warlike and ferocious, and reſembled the Scythians, from whom they were deſcended. The nation was divided into four claſſes. From the firſt they choſe their king, who was always the oldeſt of the royal family, as the next in age was general and judge; the ſecond claſs was that of the prieſts, who were alſo their ambaſſadors; the third claſs were ſoldiers and huſbandmen, and the fourth, ſlaves. Each family poſſeſſed an undivided property, which was managed by its eldeſt individual.

Beyond the river Alazonius, and from thence to the Caſpian, was the country of the Albani. Theſe were an original people; ſimple, fimple, honeft, unacquainted with money, or with exact weights and meafures, and unable to reckon beyond an hundred. For the purpofes of agriculture, they had only wooden ploughs. A fine climate, a rich foil, producing fpontaneoufly all kinds of fruits, and particularly grapes, rendered induftry unneceffary, and they fubfifted by the produce of their numerous herds which they fed on the fertile banks of the Cyrus. They were the handfomeft of mankind, and brave, though inoffenfive. They fought both on foot and horfeback, with light or heavy armour, and brought into the field againft *Pompey* an army of feventy thoufand infantry, and twenty-two thoufand horfe. Their arms were javelins, and bows and arrows, with leathern fhields, breaft-plates, and helmets. The Albani were compofed of twenty-fix tribes, each diftinguifhed by a different language, and governed by an independent prince. They adored the fun, and Jupiter, but more particularly the moon, to whom they offered human facrifices with many fuperftitious ceremonies. Their chief-prieft was next in dignity to the prince of each tribe. They had the higheft refpect for old age. They buried their dead with all their property, and then thought no more about them, not even daring to mention their names, as this was re- puted a kind of facrilege *.

In the high mountains above the Albani were the Legæ, and beyond them the fabulous nation of the Amazons. Befides thefe,

---

* This fuperftition exifts among the prefent Samoyedes,

these, many other nations are enumerated by *Strabo*, *Pliny*, and others, as the Amardi*, the Cicianthi, the Agedi, the Gabri, the Tagori, the Ifli, the Effedones, and many more; but this long catalogue of names is not accompanied by any account of their history or manners. The languages of Caucasus were supposed to be almost innumerable, since at Dioscurias alone they reckoned seventy dialects, and, according to some authors, three hundred. The Romans, indeed, seem to have known very little of this country, excepting what they learnt from the officers of *Pompey*, who entered it from Armenia, fought the Albani and Iberi, and then advanced in pursuit of *Mithridates* as far as the mouth of the Phasis, where he found *Servilius* with the Roman fleet.

AFTER the establishment of the eastern empire, the countries of Lazica (Colchis) and Iberia, were so frequently a subject of dispute between the Greek Emperors and the kings of Persia, that we might expect from the Byzantine writers a fuller and more correct account of the Caucasian nations. But the Greek historians (if we except the Emperor *Constantine*) were so ill informed

---

* It has been observed by travellers, that barbarous nations generally distinguish themselves by a name expressing *man*, and denote the rest of mankind by some degrading appellation. Supposing this custom to have prevailed in Mount Caucasus, the Amardi may have been a tribe of Armenians, in whose language *mard* signifies man. In that of the Offi, it is *leg*, and it may have been a tribe of these people who were called Legæ. The Tagori were perhaps the Dugoreans. In the language of the Circassians, man is called Tsoog, and in that of the Abkhas, Agoo: these nations occupy the county of the Ζυχοι and Αχαιοι.

informed of the geography of thefe barbarous countries, and
fo fond of comprehending all Barbarians under the collective
appellations of Huns or Turks, that their relations are never
fatisfactory, and fometimes quite unintelligible. Since their
time we have had nothing to truft to but the reports of a few
cafual travellers, until the reign of the prefent Emprefs of
Ruffia, by whom Profeffor *Guldenflaedt* was fent to mount
Caucafus, with orders to traverfe thefe wild regions in various
directions, to trace their rivers to their fources, to take aftrono-
mical obfervations, to examine the natural hiftory of the country, and to collect vocabularies of all the dialects he might meet
with, which might be afterwards referred to their refpective
languages, fo as to form a general claffification of all the nations
comprehended between the Euxine and Cafpian.

FROM the refearches of this traveller it appears that there are
in this diftrict of country at leaft feven diftinct nations, each
fpeaking a feparate language, viz. 1. The Tartars. 2. The
Abchas. 3. The Circaffians. 4. The Offi, or Offeti. 5. The
Kifti. 6. The Lefguis. 7. The Georgians. Befides thefe, the
people of Imeretia, Suaneti, and particularly thofe of Touchet,
fpeak fuch corrupt dialects of the Georgian as to make it doubt-
ful whether they ought to be referred to that language. Some
tribes of Lefguis likewife, as thofe of Andi, Akoufcha, and the
Kazi Coumyks, fpeak dialects extremely degenerated from the
original language.

The

The Tartars are of three tribes, viz.

1. Terekemens, Turcomans, or Trukhmenians. Thefe fpeak the Turkifh dialect of the Tartar language, and inhabit the eaftern flope of Caucafus, the coaft of the Cafpian about Boinak, Derbent, and Utemifh, and the fouthern promontories between the fea and the river Alazan. Their diftricts are Cuba, Altipara, Tokufpara, Mifkindfhal, Khinakug. Krifhbudug, Shamakhi, and the whole of Shirvan. They are fubject to Feth-ali, the Khan of Cuba, whofe authority extends as far as Sallian. To the weftward of thefe are the Trukmenian diftricts of Shakhi, Caballà, Agdotfh, and Arafh. Their chief is Huffein Khan, who refides at Nukhu. Laftly, there is the diftrict of Kafak, in the dominions of the king of Georgia. This lies about the rivers Nakhatyr, Tebete, Kura, Akhiftafa, and Alghete.

2. Coumyks. Thefe live to the northward of the former, about the lower parts of the rivers Sundfha, Koifu, and Axai. They are governed by a number of fmall chiefs, conftantly at variance with each other, but all profeffing allegiance to Ruffia. Bragun, Endery, and Koftek, are their chief villages.

3. Nogays. Some wandering Hordes of Nogays are difperfed among the Coumyks, but differ from them in dialect. Eight of thefe Hordes are fubject to the prince of Axai; twelve to that of Endery; and twenty-four to the Shamkhal, who refides

2

at Tarku. About a thousand families submitted to Russia in the reign of *Peter* the First, and are established along the northern side of the Terck.

A more considerable body of Nogays is that established on the Cuban, in the following divisions:—Kassai Aaul, consisting of 8000 families, encamped between the rivers Inshik and Laba, which fall into the Cuban. Naurus Aaul, of 2000 families, dwelling in permanent villages about the river Laba. Jedissan, Jedishkul, Dshamboiluk, and Akermen, filling the whole plain from the Laba to the Black Sea, along the Cuban. These Nogays retired hither on the conquest of the kingdom of Astrachan, afterwards removed to the Dnieper and Boug, and were re-admitted to their present habitations on their submission to Russia during the last war.

Besides these, there are several villages in the higher parts of Caucasus, whose inhabitants are apparently of Nogay origin, since they speak that dialect*. These districts are, 1. Malkar, of about 1000 families, on the rivers Argudan and Tsherck. This district borders to the east on the district of Dugor, to the S. W. on the Imeretian district of Radsha, and to the north on the Circassian district of Kashkatan. 2. Bisnighe, near the Tsherck, about 100 families. 3. Khulam, near the same river, and

---

* Guldenstaedt calls these districts the *province of Basiania.*

and containing about the fame number. 4. Tſhegem, about 360 families. 5. Karatchai, or Karadſhiki, near the fources of the Cuban, about 200 families.

It is not known at what period thefe Nogays took poſſeſſion of the country they at prefent occupy. The general eſtabliſhment of the Tartars in mount Caucafus is to be referred to the reign of Zingis and his immediate fucceſſors. The Tartars of Kafak, in Georgia, were probably fubjects of the unfortunate *Mehemed*, Sultan of Carizme.

II. The ABKHAS.

The principal and moſt ancient eſtabliſhments of this nation are on the fouthern ſlope of the mountains comprehended between the Cuban and the Black Sea. Thefe are tributary to the Turks, and are divided into two governments, the weſtern and eaſtern ; each fubject to a Baſha, commonly chofen out of the principal native families, one of whom refides at Sotchuk-kalé, and the other at Soghum-kalé. Their diſtricts are Shap-fick, Ubuk, Tubi, Aipga, Sads, Tſhadſhi, and Chirpis. The capital is Anacopir (formerly Nicopfis). Other remarkable places are Anaclea (formerly Heraclea) a ſtrong hold near the mouth of the Euguri. Bitchwinta, or Pityunta (formerly Pityus magna) at the mouth of the Kabeti : Bedga, Siakwi, Drandeli (formerly Dandari) old epifcopal feats ; Ilori, Kodri, Tſhomi, Zalumka, Zupu, and Bovudiak, along the fea-fhore ; and Dſhanketahabla,

D   a large a large village on the river Pſhaga, along which it extends in ſcattered houſes for near fifteen miles. Theſe Abkhas are called by the Circaſſians Kuſh-haſip, or Tranſmontani.

THE north-eaſtern and ſmalleſt diviſion of this nation is called by the Circaſſians Tapanta, and by the Tartars Altckeſek (ſix parts). Theſe Abkhas were permitted to ſettle in the laſt century between the Circaſſians of the Cabardas and thoſe of Beſlen, &c. and became ſubject to the Cabardians, who divided them under ſix families. Their diſtricts are Kiſilbek, Tam, She-gray, and Barokai, of 300 families. Baſhilbai of 1000, and Sabai. The Abkhas ſpeak an original language, eſſentially diffe-rent from all the known languages, though appearing to have a very remote affinity with that of the Circaſſians. Their coun-try is called by themſelves *Abſne;* by the Tartars, Turks, and Circaſſians, Abaſa; and by the Georgians, Abchaſeti. It is the Abaſgia of the Byzantine hiſtorians, and the Abargia of the Em-peror *Conſtantine.* The Abkhas have at preſent very little reli-gion, although they ſtill preſerve ſome traces of Chriſtianity.

III. The TSHERKESS, or CIRCASSIANS.

THESE people occupy the following diſtricts:—1. The Great Cabarda. 2. The Little Cabarda. 3. Beſlen, on the greater Laba, which falls into the Cuban. 4. Temirgoi, upon the Shagwaſha. 5. Abaſech, principally on the river Pſchaha. 6. Bſeduch,

6. Bſeduch, on the lower part of the Chuaſh: 7. Hatukai. And 8. Bſhana, on the rivers Churſa and Korkoi.

THIS nation, from the extent of their territory, which comprehends nearly ten degrees of longitude, and from their extraordinary courage and military genius, might become very formidable, were they united under one chief. But a nation of mountaineers, who ſubſiſt by raiſing cattle, and are therefore forced to eſtabliſh themſelves on the banks of rivers for the ſake of water and paſturage, ſoon forget their common origin, and divide into ſeparate and hoſtile tribes. From this principle of diſunion, the Circaſſians of the Cuban are ſo little powerful, as to be ſcarcely known even to the Ruſſians, but by the general appellation of Cuban Tartars, in which they are confounded with the Abkhas and Nogays, their neighbours.

THE Cabardian Circaſſians, however, though diſunited from the reſt of their countrymen, are ſtill the moſt powerful people of the northern ſide of Caucaſus, and this ſuperiority has introduced among their neighbours ſuch a general imitation of their manners, that from a deſcription of theſe we ſhall acquire a general idea of all the reſt: beſides which, the ſingularity of many of their cuſtoms, and their reſemblance to thoſe of the moſt ancient inhabitants of theſe countries, renders them an object of particular curioſity.

THE

THE Circaffians are divided into three claffes. 1. The Princes. 2. The Nobles (called Ufdens). And 3. The Vaffals, or People. A certain number of the people is allotted to each princely family: thus the Great Cabarda is divided in three equal portions among the three families of Giambulak, Moifauoft, and Atafhuk. In each of thefe the eldeft individual is confidered as chief of the family, and as judge, protector, and father of all the vaffals attached to it. No prince can be a landholder: he has no other property than his arms, his horfes, his flaves, and the tribute he may be able to extort from the neighbouring nations. The perfon not only of the chief, but of every prince, is facred; and this extraordinary privilege extends even to the princes of the Crimea. This is, however, the only diftinction of birth when unaccompanied by perfonal merit. The greateft honour a prince can acquire is that of being the firft of the nation to charge the enemy. The prefent poffeffor of this privilege is faid to have acquired it by an action of ftrange temerity: he undertook, with three comrades, to cut his way through a Ruffian column, and fucceeded: his companions loft their lives in this brilliant, but ufelefs enterprize. The princes are not to be diftinguifhed in time of peace from the nobles, or even from the peafants: their food and drefs are the fame, and their houfes little better.

THE Ufdens, or nobles, are chofen by the princes from the inferior clafs. They are the officers of the prince, and executors of the laws, and are employed in the general affemblies of

2   the

the nation to gain the affent of the people to the meafures propofed by the princes.

THE people, as well as the Ufdens, are proprietors of lands.
By an odd kind of contradiction, the princes claim, and fometimes attempt to exercife the right of feizing the whole property
of their vaffals; but at the fame time the vaffal has a right of
transferring his allegiance to any other prince, whenever he thinks
himfelf aggrieved : by this privilege the princes are compelled
to gain the affections of their vaffals, on whofe readinefs to follow them into the field, all their hopes of greatnefs and wealth
muft abfolutely depend.

THE Circaffians do not appear to have ever had any written
laws, but are governed by a kind of common law, or collection
of ancient ufages.　On great occafions the whole nation is
affembled : a meafure is propofed by the oldeft of the princes,
and this meafure is firft debated among the Ufdens, and afterwards by the deputies of the people, who are old men, elected
for this purpofe, and who often poffefs greater weight and in-
fluence over the people than even the prince himfelf.　If the
propofition is accepted, it becomes a national refolution, and is
confirmed by a folemn oath by. the whole people.　This ceremony generally takes place on a fpot particularly deftined to the
purpofe near the refidence of the prince.

THE

THE Circaffians have few manufactures. The points of their arrows are the only articles of iron which they work up themfelves. They make, indeed, fome very fine cloths, and felt for cloaks, which is uncommonly light and durable; and to thefe we may add, a few articles of leather, embroidered houfings for horfes, &c. Their coats of mail, which are very beautiful, are bought from Perfia, and their fire-arms from Kubefcha. Their agriculture produces barely, what is fufficient for their own fubfiftence. Sheep and horfes are the principal articles of their commerce, particularly the latter, which fell at a very high price; but notwithftanding this, the balance of trade would be confiderably againft them, were it not for the flaves which they make in their predatory excurfions. The art of conducting thefe expeditions is therefore the moft valuable talent of a Cir-caffian prince, and the great object of a long and painful education.

AT the birth of a prince, fome Ufden, or fometimes a prince of another family is chofen by the father as his future preceptor. At a year old he is prefented, at the fame time, with fome play-things and arms: if he appears to prefer the latter, the event is celebrated in the family by great rejoicings. At feven (or according to others, at twelve) years of age he leaves his father's houfe for that of his preceptor. By him he is taught to ride, to ufe his arms, and to fteal, and conceal his thefts. The word thief is a term of the utmoft reproach amongft them, becaufe it

implies

implies detection. He is afterwards led to more confiderable and dangerous robberies, and does not return to his father's houfe, until his cunning, his addrefs, and his ftrength are fuppofed to be perfect. The preceptor is recompenfed for his trouble by nine-tenths of the booty made by his pupil while under his tuition. It is faid that this mode of education is perfevered in with a view to prevent the bad effects of paternal indulgence. The cuftom is, I believe, peculiar to the Circaffians, but the object of education is the fame among all the mountaineers of Caucafus, who univerfally fubfift by robbery, for which reafon the accounts of their ferocity appear to have been greatly exaggerated. Wars have been frequently undertaken with no other view but that of plunder, by nations who call themfelves highly civilized, and fuch wars have not been confidered as an impeachment of their humanity. In anfwer to the complaints of travellers, the princes of thefe little tribes might urge that the fecrecy of their retreats is to them highly important; that they have in common with all fovereigns a right to punifh fpies and enemies; that to pillage or enflave fuch merchants as travel through their country without their permiffion is not more cruel than to condemn the contraband trader to death or to the galleys; and while they receive with difinterefted hofpitality and kindnefs fuch as court their protection, they might declaim in their turn againft the methodical extortions of European cuftom-houfes.

THE education of a child renders the preceptor a kind of adopted

adopted father; therefore, as this is a very vindictive nation, a person who has killed any prince, endeavours by all the means in his power to steal away some child of the same family in order to educate him. The accomplishment of this is the only sure means of effecting a reconciliation. Some travellers report that a vaſſal ſometimes contrives to ſteal and educate the ſon of his prince, and by his ſucceſs inſures his own advancement to nobility. The point in which all agree is the neceſſity that the child ſhould be educated at a diſtance from the father.

GIRLS are brought up by the mother. They learn to em-broider, to make their own dreſs, and that of their future huſbands. The daughters of ſlaves receive the ſame education, and are ſold according to their beauty, from twenty to one hun-dred pounds, and ſometimes much higher. Theſe are princi-pally Georgians. Soon after the birth of a girl a wide leather belt is ſewed round her waiſt, and continues till it burſts, when it is replaced by a ſecond. By a repetition of this practice their waiſts are rendered aſtoniſhingly ſmall, but their ſhoulders be-come proportionably broad : a defect which is little attended to on account of the beauty of their breaſts. On the wedding night the belt is cut with a dagger by the huſband, a cuſtom ſometimes productive of very fatal accidents. The bridegroom pays for his bride a marriage preſent, or kalym, conſiſting of arms or a coat of mail, but he muſt not ſee her, or cohabit with her, without

the

the greateſt myſtery. This reſerve continues during life. A Circaſſian will ſometimes permit a ſtranger to ſee his wife, but he muſt not accompany him. The father makes the bride a preſent on the wedding day, but reſerves the greater part of what he intends to give her till the birth of her firſt child. On this occaſion ſhe pays him a viſit, receives from him the remainder of her portion, and is cloathed by him in the dreſs of a matron, the principal diſtinction of which conſiſts in a veil. Until this time the dreſs of the women is much like that of the men, excepting that the cloak is longer, and frequently white, a colour never worn by men. The cap too is generally red, or roſe-coloured.

BEFORE marriage the youth of both ſexes ſee each other freely at the little rejoicings which take place on feſtivals. Before the ball, the young men ſhew their activity and addreſs in a variety of military exerciſes, and the moſt alert have the privilege of chuſing the moſt beautiful partners. Their muſical inſtruments are a long flute with only three ſtops, a ſpecies of mandoline, and a tambourin. Their dances are in the Aſiatic ſtile, with very little gaiety or expreſſion. The ſteps ſeem very difficult, but not graceful.

THE Circaſſian women participate in the general character of the nation; they take pride in the courage of their huſbands, and reproach them ſeverely when defeated. They poliſh and take care of the armour of the men. Widows tear their hair,

E

and

and disfigure themfelves with fcars, in teftimony of their grief. The men had formerly the fame cuftom, but are now grown more tranquil, under the lofs of their wives and relations. The habitation of a Circaffian is compofed of two huts, becaufe the wife and hufband are not fuppofed to live together. One of thefe huts is allotted to the hufband, and to the reception of ftrangers; the other to the wife and family: the court which feparates them is furrounded by palifades or ftakes. At meals the whole family is affembled; fo that here, as among the Tartars, each village is reckoned at a certain number of kettles. Their food is extremely fimple, confifting only of a little meat, fome pafte made of millet, and a kind of beer, compofed of the fame grain fermented.

THE Circaffians are accufed of frequent perjuries and violations of treaties; but this is faid to be a new vice among them. Whatever may have been the original religion of this people, they have been fucceffively converted to Chriftianity and Mahometanifm, and have now no religion or worfhip among them. They break, without fcruple, fuch oaths as they have taken on the Bible and Alcoran; but there are certain forms of oaths, and certain places in the neighbourhood of their ruins (fuppofed to be remains of Chriftian churches) which infure their fidelity *.

Their

* This is not improbable. In 1726, the Ruffians reinftated a Khan of Cuba, and forced his fubjects to take the oath of allegiance to him. Being Mahometans, they fwore on the Alcoran;

Their courage, great as it is, is not yet proof againſt religious terrors. Like all Barbarians, they believe that what is called accident may be influenced by particular ceremonies. In an action with the Ruſſians a Circaſſian prince happened to be ſhot. A Coſak of Kiſlar, acquainted with the rites of the Circaſſians, inſtantly ran to the body, opened it, plucked out the heart, and running with it to a river, and carefully waſhing it, threw it from him to ſome diſtance in the direction of the ſtream, with the moſt violent imprecations. He conceived that by this ceremony he had ſecured the victory to the Ruſſians. A ſacrifice performed by the people of Tchetchen ſeems more analogous to common ſuperſtition. The day after a bloody engagement, in which they had been ſucceſsful, they led a Ruſſian priſoner to the field of battle, where they put him to death, as a ſacrifice to the ſpirits of their ſlaughtered countrymen, and as an atonement to heaven for the blood that had been ſpilt on the preceding day.

It is not extraordinary that the freedom of their goverment, the martial ſpirit of their women, their habitual abſtinence, and familiarity with danger, ſhould render the Circaſſians a moſt dangerous enemy to the undiſciplined Georgians, but their ingenuity in war has rendered them formidable even to regular

troops.

Alcoran; but it was ſuggeſted to the Ruſſians, that it was neceſſary that each man ſhould likewiſe bind himſelf by the following imprecation :—" May my wife become a proſtitute, " and may I be diſhonoured by every man, if I break this oath !"—*Gaerber's Narrative.*

troops. In one of their actions against the Ruffians, they arrived in the field, pushing before them a kind of moveable rampart against which the artillery had no effect. They had adjusted between the wheels of their carts a fort of drum, compofed of fafcines, wool, and other foft fubftances, and covered with fkins. Thefe machines, being moveable, oppofed fcarcely any refiftance to the balls, which penetrated and lodged in them without doing any damage. After a long engagement, in which the Ruffians loft a number of men from the well-directed fire of the enemy, they attacked this intrenchment with fixed bayonets, and forced the Circaffians to retire.

The Circaffians have not any letters of their own; thofe among them who wifh to write their language being obliged to make ufe of Arabian characters. We are told, indeed, that on fome remains of tomb-ftones, in their mountains, are infcriptions, now unintelligible; and their princes pretend that they are in poffeffion of certain old books, containing the hiftory and antiquities of their nation. Thefe laft, however, are perhaps nothing more than devotional manufcripts left among them either by the Chriftian or Mahometan priefts, whofe religions they have fucceffively embraced and deferted, fo that their ancient hiftory muft now reft almoft folely on conjecture. From the name which they give themfelves, Adige, it is poffible that they may be the fame with the Agedi, a people mentioned by *Pliny* among the Caucafian nations: and at a later period they feem to have been comprehended with many neighbouring people, under the name of Alani, to have been subjugated by the Huns, and laftly by the Khazari, a nation of Tartar origin, with whom they were incorporated under the name of Cabari.

We are told, by the emperor *Conftantine*, that thefe Cabari, upon feme difagreement with the reft of the Khazar tribes had recourfe to arms, but were defeated; and that the vanquifhed tribe divided into two parts, one of which retreated towards the neighbourhood of Perfia, which at that time was in the hands of the Arabians, and comprehended the greater part of Iberia. This divifion probably gave its name to the two Cabardas. The other retired to the Hungarians (called Turks* in *Conftantine*'s relation) and formed an eftablifhment on the frontiers of the Kherfonitæ. From thefe the river Cabarta and the ruined fort of Tfherkefs-Kerman, in the vicinity of the ancient

---

* The Greek hiftorians, in imitation of the Perfians, gave the name of Turks to all thofe northern Barbarians whom they had before confounded with the Huns. The firft Turks, according to *Theophanes*, were the Kermikhiones, who fubdued the Kerkhis and Seres (probably the Kirguis and Boukharians). They lived to the eaftward of the Don (ϖρος τερον ανεμον του Ταναιδος) and the refidence of their prince was at a mountain called Ek-Tal, fignifying in their language the golden mountain, and fo called from the richnefs of its paftures. This word feems to belong to the Syrainifh (a Finnifh dialect) in which Effifh fignifies gold, and Tfhol a mountain.

The name of Turk is equally given to the Hungarians (whofe language is of Finnifh origin) and to the Khazars, who were perhaps a Tartar race. *Abulgafi* (the Tartar hiftorian) applies the name indifferently to all the Mongul as well as Tartar tribes, while the prefent Europeans ufe it for the Othman Tartars only.

ancient Kherfon, may perhaps have derived their name. It is obferved by M. *Peyffonel*, that the Hungarian language contains feveral Circaffian words, a circumftance which feems to confirm what is here related, and which indeed correfponds very nearly with the tradition of the Circaffian Princes concerning their own origin. This is in fubftance as follows. " They are derived from a certain Prince of the name of *Kefs*, who in former times was eftablifhed in the Crimea. This prince had two fons, *Inal* and *Chaombok*. The elder fons of *Inal* had a numerous progeny, who, towards the clofe of the laft century, were all affaffinated in a general infurrection of the nation, produced by their haughtinefs and cruelty. From the younger fons of *Inal* are defcended the prefent princes of the Cuban Circaffians, and from *Chaombok* the three families who now govern the Cabardas. Prince *Kefs*, and his immediate defcendants, were defpotic; but the increafe of their numbers, and confequent diminution of their authority, produced that mixed form of government which fubfifts at this day."

FROM this tradition, which relates only to the princely families, it feems that they are of a different origin from their fubjects; indeed the fame thing feems to be evinced by the fuperftitious reverence with which they are treated, and which, among uncivilized nations, is feldom claimed but by conquerors from the conquered people. Befides, the fame tradition concern-

2   ing

ing prince *Kefs* and his fon *Inal*, fubfifts among the Kirguis
Tartars, in whofe language the word Kefs fignifies man.

FROM the eighth century to the twelfth, the Circaffians are
only mentioned, by the Greek and Ruffian hiftorians, under the
name of *Cafaks**, an appellation which is ftill given to them by
their neighbours the Offi. By the Arabians they were ufually
called Mamlouks †, and, by the Georgians, Tfherkeffiani, from
whence the Tartars and Europeans perhaps borrowed the name
of Tfherkefs, and Circaffians, by which they have been generally
known. After the declenfion of the Khazar empire, they appear to have been fucceffively fubject to the Arabians, as mafters
of Perfia, to the Tartars, and perhaps to the Georgians; and
towards the clofe of the fixteenth century they became tributary
to Ruffia. In 1560, the Tfar *Ivan Vaffilievitch*, married *Maria*,
daughter

---

* The flat countries, near the Volga, were always called by the Tartars Capchak, which
Strahlenburg fuppofes to have been corrupted into Cafaccia, and Cafak. Hence the names of
the Cafaccia Orda, or Kerguis Cafaks, the diftrict of Cafaccia (placed by *Conftantine* near
the Cuban, and now inhabited by the Circaffians) the Turcoman Cafaks in Georgia, near
the river Kura, the Don and Zaporavian Cafaks, &c. &c.

† M. *Volney* (Voyage en Syrie et en Egypte, vol. I. p. 90) has given a very circumftantial
account of the Caucafian militia, who, under the name of Mamlouks, or military flaves, are
the mafters of Egypt. The following affertion is very curious :—" Depuis cinq cent cin-
quante ans qu' il y a des Mamlouks en Egypte, *pas un feul* n'a donné lignée fubfiftante; il
n'en exifte pas une famille à la feconde generation, *tous leurs enfans periffent* dans le premier
ou le fecond age."—" Le moyen qui les a perpetués eft donc le meme qui les y a etablis : c'eft
a dire, qu'ils fe font régénerés par des efclaves tranfportes de leur pays originel." If this be
true, the Ruffians have rendered a moft important fervice to the Turkifh government by
checking the traffic of flaves in Mount Caucafus.

daughter of *Temruk*, a prince of Circaflia, who had fent her as an hoftage to Mofcow, where fhe embraced the Greek religion. Five years afterwards, the Tfar fent a fmall army, under the command of General *Dafhkow*, to the affiftance of *Temruk*; but after the death of *Ivan*, thefe diftant fubjects feem to have been forgotten by the court of Ruffia; in confequence of which negligence, the Khans of the Crimea, as heirs of the Tartar empire, laid claim to the fovereignty of thefe countries, and eafily induced the Circaffians to pay them a fmall tribute as the price of their protection. But the officers of the Khan, under pretence of levying this tribute, having been guilty of great exceffes, infulting the wives and daughters of the Circaffians, and treating them in every refpect like a conquered nation, they took up arms, murdered the collectors, and foon after cut to pieces an army of thirty thoufand Tartars, who had been fent by the Khan to punifh them for their difobedience. This happened at the beginning of the prefent century.

THE foregoing defcription of the Circaffians, as far as relates to the free fpirit of their government, their general modes of life, and many of their particular cuftoms, is equally applicable to all the mountaineers of Caucafus, and probably to every uncivilized nation upon earth. But two of their cuftoms feem peculiar to themfelves. The one, by which the hufbands are prohibited, under pain of infamy, from publickly converfing with their wives, fo that the two fexes are divided as it were

into

into two diftinct communities ;—the other, by which the education of all male children is entrufted to ftrangers in preference
to the parents, the females only being brought up by their mo-
thers. It is not eafy to conceive from what diftant nation thefe
ftrange regulations can be derived ; and if we fuppofe them to
have exifted at an early period in mount Caucafus, they may
perhaps account in fome meafure for the fabulous defcription of
the Amazons and Gargarenfes, who are placed by ancient geographers in the country now occupied by the Circaffians *.

F   IV. The

* *Strabo* obferves on this ftory, that whereas other fictions of antiquity had gradually fallen
into contempt, this alone continued to be confirmed by the teftimonies of fucceeding travellers. Indeed, it is not very extraordinary that women fhould be employed in tending
horfes, or in riding them afterwards, or that they fhould attend their hufbands to battle.
Procopius relates, that the Romans, after a battle with the Huns, frequently found among the
flain the bodies of women. *Zonaras* fays, that after the engagement of *Pompey* with the Albani, there were found feveral fuits of armour belonging to the Amazons. While father
Lamberti was in Mingrelia, the Dadian (or prince of the country) received the account of
an irruption of fome Caucafian tribes, who had attacked the Suani and Caraccioli (people of
Karatchai). They were repulfed, and many bodies of women were found on the field of
battle. The armour of thefe women was prefented to the Dadian, and confifted of helmets,
braffards, and cuiraffes, made of fmall fteel plates. To the cuirafs was faftened a kind of
petticoat which reached about half way down the legs, made of ferge, of a moft beautiful
red. (Recueil de Voyages au Nord, vol. x. p. 180). The moft wonderful parts of the ancient ftory are, the myfterious commerce of the Amazons with their temporary hufbands, the
Gargarenfes—their mode of difpofing of their male children—and the amputation performed
on the breafts of the females, which laft circumftance was probably invented by the Greek
etymologifts in order to explain the name of the nation. Perhaps it might not be more ab-
furd to derive that name from the Circaffian word Maza, the moon, which is reported to
have been the favourite deity of the mountaineers of Caucafus, than from the Greek word
Μαζον, which fignifies a woman's breaft ; but this muft reft for the decifion of etymologifts.

IV. The OSSI, or OSSETI.

THE northern divifion of this nation is fcattered about the rivulets that fall into the Terek, as far as the Lefken. The fouthern is fettled on the Aragui, the Kfani, the two Liakwis,. which fall into the Kura, and the Dfhedfho, that joins the Kion. Their diftricts are,

1. Saka, Nar, Sannach, and Walagir, upon the river Aredon.

2. Dughor, near the rivers Dughor and Urukh.

3 Kewi, and Kefuri, alfo called Soni and Mekeweni, on the rivulets that fall into the Kumbelei and Terek.

4. Gelaxan, on the Kumbelei.

5. Kurtat, or Kurtauli, at the fource of the Pogh..

6. Guda, about the fources of the Aragui.

7. Saperfcheti, between the Kfani and Aragui.

8. Wanati, Tfhamuri, and Lomifa, about the fource of the Kfani.

9. Tagata, or Tagae-ur, about the Kizel and Terek.

10. Tirfan, or Trufo, about the upper part of the Terek.

11. Archoti, near the Kumbelei.

12. Makal, in the Offetin language Komoiti, below the former, near the Terek.

13. Gnafur, Tkupta, Padfhur, Kobais, Ghria, Tfghru, and Guugho, along the Batara Liakwi.

14 Ruka,

14. Ruka, at the fource of the Didi Liakwi.

15. Dfhaukom, on the Paza that joins the Didi Liakwi. This is a large and very populous diftrict, containing more than a thoufand families.

16. Urdfwalda, called by the Georgians Magran-Dwaleti, near the fame river.

17. Birtaul, on a river of the fame name that falls into the Liakwi.

18. Sgobir, Dfhiwatfkur, and Dfhomach, about the upper part of the Didi Liakwi.

19. Dwaleti, about the Dfhedfho that joins the Rion.

THIS laft diftrict is fubject to the prince of Imeretia; the others are fubject to that of Georgia. Thefe diftricts are of very unequal fize, fome containing only five, and others fifty villages, each of which comprifes from twenty to an hundred families.

THE Offi are by the Circaffians and Tartars called Kufha, i. e. Bones. They call themfelves by the different appellations of Jir, Walp, Ghuatan, and Gherolin. *Guldenftaedt* thinks them the remainder of the Uzi, or Polowzi. Their language has fome analogy with the Perfian; the Dugorian feems even to be a dialect of that language. Their hiftory is entirely unknown.

V. The

V. The KISTI.*

THIS nation extends from the higheſt ridge of Caucaſus, along the Sundſha rivulets. They are bounded to the weſt by the little Cabarda, to the eaſt by the Tartars and Leſguis, and to the ſouth by the Leſguis and Georgians. Their diſtricts are,

1. Inguſhi,† about 60 miles to the ſouthward of Moſdok, in the

---

* Theſe may perhaps be the people whom *Gaerber* calls the Taulinzi (i. e. mountaineers) and to whom he attributes the following ſtrange cuſtom :—" When a gueſt or ſtranger comes to lodge with them, one of the hoſt's daughters is obliged to receive him, to unſaddle and feed his horſe, take care of his baggage, prepare his dinner, paſs the night with him, and continue at his diſpoſal during his ſtay. At his departure, ſhe ſaddles his horſe and packs up his baggage. It would be very uncourtly to refuſe any of theſe marks of hoſpitality." *Priſcus*, I believe, relates that, during his travels among the Huns, he once received ſome offers of this ſort, which he thought proper to decline.

† The Inguſhi are capable of arming about 5000 men. They call themſelves Inguſhi, Kiſti, or Halha. They live in villages near each other, containing about 20 or 30 houſes; are diligent huſbandmen, and rich in cattle. Many of their villages have a ſtone tower, which ſerves in time of war as a retreat to their women and children, and as a magazine for their effects. Theſe people are all armed, and have the cuſtom of wearing ſhields.

Their religion is very ſimple, but has ſome traces of Chriſtianity. They believe in one God, whom they call Dailé, but have no ſaints or religious perſons. They celebrate Sunday, not by any religious ceremony, but by reſting from labour. They have a faſt in ſpring, and another in ſummer. They obſerve no ceremonies either at births or deaths. They allow of poligamy, and eat pork. One kind of ſacrifice is uſual among them : at certain times a ſheep is killed by a perſon who ſeems to be conſidered as a kind of prieſt, as he is obliged to live in a ſtate of celibacy. His habitation is in the mountains, near an old ſtone church, which is ſaid to be adorned with various ſtatues and inſcriptions. Under the church is a vault that contains certain old books, which, however, no one ever attempts to approach. Mr. *Guldenſtaedt* was prevented by the weather from viſiting this church. (*Guldenſtaedt's* Reiſe, vol. I. page 150.)

the high mountains about the Kumbelei. This tribe fubmitted to Ruffia in 1770.

2. Endery, and 3. Axai, on a low ridge between the Sundfha and Iaxai rivers. In their territories are the hotwells.

4. Ackinyurt, towards the upper part of the Sundfha and Kumbelei.

5. Ardakli, on the Rofhni that joins the Sundfha.

6. Wapi, near the Offetin village Tfhim, towards the fource of the Terek.

7. Angufht, on the upper part of the Kumbelei.

8. Shalkha, called by the Ruffians Maloi Angufht. This, and the two preceding tribes, which were formerly tributary to the Cabardian princes, fubmitted to Ruffia in 1770.

9. Tfhetfhen, on the lower part of the Argun river. It is governed by its own chiefs, who are related to the Avar-Khan. This tribe is fo numerous and warlike, and has given the Ruffians fo much trouble, that its name is ufually given by them to the whole Kifti nation. The chief village of Tihetfhen lies on the Argun, about 15 miles from its mouth. Its other principal villages are Hadfhi-aul, and Iangejent, both on the Sundfha.

10. Atakhi, a fmall diftrict on the upper part of the Argun.

11. Kulga, or Dfhanti, in the high mountains.

12. Galgai, or Halha, about the fource of the Afai, a Sundfha rivulet.

13. Tfhabrilo, and Shabul, on the Sundfha.

14. Tfhifhni-Kabul, on the Rofhni, a Sundfha rivulet.

15. Kara-

15. Karaboulak, a wandering tribe, who have their little villages about the fix uppermoft rivulets of the Sundfha, particularly the Fortan.

16. Meefti, Meredfhi, Galafhka, and Duban; thefe are fmall tribes on the Axai.

THE different tribes of this reftlefs and turbulent nation are generally at variance with each other, and with all their neighbours. Their dialects have no analogy with any known language, and their hiftory and origin are at prefent utterly unknown.

VI. The LESGUIS.

THE country of this people is indifferently called by the Georgians Lefguiftan, and Dagheftan. It is bounded to the S. and E. by Perfia and the Cafpian, to the S. W. and W. by Georgia, the Offi, and Kifti, and to the N. by the Kifti and Tartar tribes. It is divided into a variety of diftricts, generally independent, and governed by chiefs elected by the people. *Guldenftaedt* has remarked, in the Lefguis language, eight different dialects, and has claffed their tribes in conformity to this obfervation.

THE firft dialect comprehends fifteen tribes, which are as follow :

1. Avar, in Georgian Chunfagh. The chief of this diftrict com-

commonly called Avar-Khan, is the moſt powerful prince of Lefguiſtan, and refides at Kabuda, on the river Kaferuk. The village of Avar is, in the dialect of Andi, called Harbul.

2. Kaferuk, in the high mountains, extending along a branch of the Koifu, called Karak. This diſtrict is dependant on the Khan of the Kafi Kumychs.

3. Idatle on the Koifu, joining on the Andi; fubject to the Avar Khan.

4. Mukratle, fituated on the Karak, and fubject to the Avan Khan.

5. Onfekul, fubject to the fame, and fituated on the Koifu.

6. Karakhle, upon the Karak, below Kaferuk, fubject to the fame.

7. Ghumbet, on the river Ghumbet, that joins the Koifu, fubject to the chief of the Coumyks.

8. Arakan; and 9, Burtuma, on the Koifu.

10. Antfugh, on the Samura, fubject to Georgia.

11. Tebel, on the fame river, independent.

12. Tamurgi, or Tumural, on the fame river.

13. Akhti; and 14, Rutul, on the fame.

15. Dſhar, in a valley that runs from the Alazan to the Samura. It was formerly fubject to Georgia, but is now independent. In this diſtrict are feen remains of the old wall* that begins at Derbent, and probably terminates at the Alazan.

The

---

* The inhabitants of Derbent believe that their town was built by Alexander, and that this wall formerly extended as far as the Black Sea. It is, however, probable, from many

THE fecond dialect is fpoken in the two following diftricts :

1. Dido, or Didonli, about the fource of the Samura. This diftrict is rich in mines; a ridge of uninhabited mountains divides it from Caket.

2. Unfo, on the fmall rivulets that join the Samura. Thefe two diftricts, containing together about a thoufand families, were formerly fubject to Georgia, but are now independent.

THE third dialect is that of

Kabutfh, which lies on the Samura rivulets, caft of Dido, and north of Caket.

THE fourth dialect is that of

Andi, fituated on a rivulet that runs into the Koifu. Some of its villages are fubject to the Avar-Khan, but the greater part to the Khan of Axai. The whole confifts of about 800 families.

THE fifth dialect is common to four diftricts, namely,

1. Akufha, on the Koifu, fubject to the Ufmei,* or Khan

of

---

infcriptions in old Turkifh, Perfian, Arabic, and Rufifh characters, that the wall, and the aqueducts with their various fubterraneous paffages, many of which are now filled up, are of high antiquity. This town fuffered greatly during its fiege by Sultan *Amurath*, who entirely deftroyed the lower quarter, then inhabited by Greeks. It was again taken by Schach Abbas. (*Gaerber*). This town is the old Pylæ Cafpiæ.

* The following cuftom is attributed, by colonel *Gaerber*, to the fubjects of this prince :—
" Whenever

of the Caitaks, and Kara-Caitaks, containing about a thoufand families.

2. Balkar,

3. Kubefha,* near the Koifu; and

4. Zudakara,

" Whenever the Ufinci has a fon, he is carried round from village to village, and alternately fuckled by every woman who has a child at her breaft until he is weaned. This cuftom, by eftablifhing a kind of brotherhood between the prince and his fubjects, fingularly endears them to each other.

* Colonel *Gaerber*, who wrote an account of thefe countries in 1728, gives the following defcription of this very curious place. " Kubefha is a large, ftrong town, fituated on a hill between high mountains. Its inhabitants call themfelves Franki (Franks, a name common in the eaft to all Europeans) and relate, that their anceftors were brought hither by fome accident, the particulars of which are now forgotten. The common conjecture is, that they were mariners caft away upon the coaft; but thofe who pretend to be better verfed in their hiftory, tell the ftory this way :—The Greeks and Genoefe, fay they, carried on, during feveral centuries, a confiderable trade, not only on the Black Sea, but likewife on the Cafpian, and were certainly acquainted with the mines contained in thefe mountains, from which they drew by their trade with the inhabitants great quantities of filver, copper, and other metals. In order to work thefe upon the fpot, they fent hither a number of workmen to eftablifh manufactures, and inftruct the inhabitants. The fubfequent invafions of the Arabs, Turks, and Monguls, during which the mines were filled up, and the manufactures abandoned, prevented the ftrangers from effecting their return, fo that they continued here, and erected themfelves into a republic. What renders this account the more probable is, that they are ftill excellent artifts, and make very good fire-arms, as well rifled as plain; fabres, coats of mail, and feveral articles in gold and filver, for exportation. They have, likewife, for their own defence, fmall copper cannons, of three pounds calibre, caft by themfelves. They coin Turkifh and Perfian filver money, and even rubles, which readily pafs current, becaufe they are of the full weight and value. In their vallies they have pafture and arable lands as well as gardens; but they purchafe the greater part of their corn, trufting chiefly for fupport to the fale of their manufactures, which are much admired in Perfia, Turkey, and the Crimea. They are generally in good circumftances, are a quiet, inoffenfive people, but high-fpirited, and independent. Their town is confidered as a neutral fpot, where the neighbouring princes can depofit their treafures with fafety."

G

" They

4. Zudakara, or Zadakh, down the Koifu, fubject to the Ufmei. It contains about two thoufand families.

The fixth dialect belongs to the diftricts on the eaftern flope of Caucafus, between Tarku and Derbent, which are,

1. Caitak; and 2, Tabafferan, or Kara-Caitak, both fubject to the Ufmei.

The feventh dialect is that of Kafi-Coumyk, on a branch of the Koifu, near Zudakara.

This tribe has a Khan, whofe authority is recognized by fome neighbouring diftricts.

The eighth dialect is that of Kuracle, belonging to the Khan of Cuba.

Besides thefe, there are fome other Lefguis tribes, whofe dialects Mr. *Guldenftaedt* was unable to procure. From a comparifon of thofe which he has obtained, it appears that the language of the Lefguis has no kind of affinity with any other known

---

" They elect yearly twelve magiftrates, to whom they pay the moft unlimited obedience; and as all the inhabitants are on a footing of perfect equality, each individual is fure to have in his turn a fhare in the government. In the year 1725, their magiftrates, as well as the Ufmei, acknowledged the fovereignty of Ruffia, but without paying any tribute."

known language, excepting only the Samoyede,* to which it
has a remote refemblance.

This people is probably defcended from the tribes of mountaineers, known to ancient geographers under the name of
Lefgæ,

---

* The diftrict of Avar is generally fuppofed to have been received from the Avari, a rem-
nant of the Huns, who retired into this part of Caucafus. We fhould expect, therefore, to
find in thefe countries fome traces of their ancient language; and fince the Samoyede is the
only known language with which the Lefguis dialects have any affinity, it may be doubted
whether *Strahlenberg* was miftaken in fuppofing that the Huns were, in part at leaft, compofed
of Samoyedes.

M. de Guignes, on the contrary, is of opinion, that the Huns were the people known to
the firft Chinefe by the name of Hoang-nou; that they were of the fame origin with the
Turks, by whom they were fucceeded in the empire of Tartary; and that they were the anceftors of the prefent Monguls and Calmouks: and this opinion he grounds on the teftimony
of *Ammianus Marcellinus*, and that of the Chinefe hiftorians.

The defcription of the Huns by *Marcellinus* is, in general, applicable to all the paftoral
nations in Afia. The moft curious particulars are thofe which follow:—" Hunnorum gens—
ultra paludes Mæoticas glacialem oceanum accolens, omnem modum feritatis excedit.—*Quo-
niam fulcantur infantum altius genæ*, fenefcunt imberbes, abfque ulla venuftate—compactis omnes firmifque membris, et opimis cervicibus, prodigiofæ formæ & pandi, ut bipedes exiftimes
beftias—*aguntur autem nulla feveritate regali, fed tumultuario optimatum ductu contenti, perrum-
punt quidquid inciderit*." The cuftom of marking the cheeks is, I believe, at prefent peculiar to
the Toungoufes (a people apparently of the Mandfhour race); but it is ufed as an ornament
only, and not with a view to prevent the growth of the beard. The Calmouks refemble the
Huns in their uglinefs, their want of beards, and in the cuftom of paffing the greater part of
their lives on horfeback. In their internal difcipline they have no refemblance. Mr. *Pallas*
has obferved, that the Mongul tribes are the *only* paftoral people in northern Afia, who appear
to have been at all times fubject to an arbitrary and hereditary government. They have a
regular code of laws, and are diftinguifhed from all their neighbours by their fuperior faga-
city, frugality, and docility. It is remarkable, that a people, *exactly* refembling the Calmouks, is mentioned by *Theophylactus*, under the name of *Taugas*. Thefe, he fays, were
a noble colony of *Turks*. They were free from inteftine difcords, becaufe they were fubject

to

Lefgæ, or Ligyes. The ftrength of their country, which is a region of mountains, whofe paffes are known only to themfelves,

to *hereditary princes*. They worſhipped ſtatues, were governed by juſt laws, and diſtinguiſhed by their frugality. Ὁὃι τῆς Τατγας κλιματαρχης Ταισαν ονομαζεται. *Taidſhi* is in fact the title of the Calmouk princes.

To the teſtimony of the Chineſe hiſtorians it may be objected, that they do not ſeem to have diſcriminated between the different paſtoral nations of Aſia (who certainly have not a common origin) and that the identity of the Huns and Turks may be juſtly queſtioned. The northern regions of Siberia are inhabited by many different nations, all of whom, by their appearance, by their manners, by the diſperſed ſituation in which they are found, and by the teſtimony of their traditions, appear to have been driven thither out of Tartary during ſome of thoſe revolutions to which that country has been always ſubject. Since, therefore, the Hoang-nou were diſpoſſeſſed by the Turks, it ſeems more natural to look for their deſcendants in the place of their retreat than in the country of the victors.

The Samoyede nation is ſtrangely diſperſed : ſome of them are found in ſmall and detached bodies among the mountains which lie to the weſtward of lake Baikal ; others are ſuppoſed to be within the Chineſe frontiers ; others are ſcattered among the deſarts, which extend along the frozen ocean ; and ſome nearly as far to the weſtward as Archangel. It ſhould ſeem, therefore, that they muſt have been formerly a very numerous and powerful nation. They have no longer the uſe of horſes, becauſe the climate of their preſent country renders their ſubſiſtence impoſſible ; but they have ſtill preſerved the manners of a paſtoral people, and retain the uſe of moveable habitations, with which they wander from place to place. They neither have, nor appear to have ever had, any kind of regular government ; their traditional ſongs mention only certain heroes, who, in better times, led their anceſtors to battle. Theſe ſongs form their principal amuſement ; but the exploits they celebrate are never likely to be renewed. Whether it be owing to the ſeptic qualities of their food, to the natural effects of exceſſive cold, or to thoſe poiſonous fogs which render ſome parts of their country quite uninhabitable, the nerves of the Samoyedes are ſo irritable, that a ſudden and unexpected noiſe will frequently throw them into convulſions. Of this, profeſſor *Pallas* relates ſome remarkable inſtances.

The Samoyedes have a large head ; a flat face ; high cheek bones ; ſmall eyes ; a flat noſe ; a wide mouth ; a yellow complexion : large ears ; ſtraight, harſh, black hair ; a ſhort thick neck ; broad ſhoulders ; and ſhort and thin legs. " Les hommes (ſays *Klingſtadt* Mem. ſur les Samoyedes & Lappons) n'ont que fort peu ou preſque point de barbe, et ils ont ceci de commun avec leurs femmes, que non plus qu'elles ils n'ont du poil ſur aucune partie de leur corps, excepté a la tête."

felves, has probably at all times fecured them from foreign in-
vafion; but as the fame caufe muft have divided them into a
number of tribes, independent of each other, and perhaps always diftinguifhed by different dialects, it is not eafy to imagine
any common caufe of union which can ever have affembled the
whole nation, and have led them to undertake very remote con-
quefts. Their hiftory, therefore, were it known, would probably be very uninterefting to us. They fubfift by raifing cattle, and by predatory expeditions into the countries of their more
wealthy neighbours. During the troubles in Perfia, towards the
beginning of this century, they repeatedly facked the towns of
Shamachie and Ardebil, and ravaged the neighbouring diftricts ;
and the prefent wretched ftate of Georgia and of part of Armenia,
is owing to the frequency of their incurfions. In their perfons
and drefs, and in their general habits of life, as far as thefe are
known to us, they greatly refemble the Circaffians.

VII. The GEORGIANS.

GEORGIA, called by the Perfians Gurgiftan, and by the Turks
Gurtfhi, comprehends the ancient Iberia, Colchis, and perhaps
a part of Albania, as the province of Caket is faid to be diftinguifhed, in the old Georgian language, by the name of Albon.
The inhabitants are Chriftians of the Greek communion, and appear to have received their prefent name from their attachment to
St. George, the tutelary Saint of thefe countries.

GEORGIA is divided into nine provinces, 1, Semo Kartveli, or upper Carduel; 2. Kueme Kartveli, or lower Carduel; 3. Somgheti; 4. Kakheti; 5. Tſhina-kartveli, or inner Carduel; 6. Imereti; 7. Guria; 8. Suaneti; and 9. Mingreli. Of theſe, the five firſt are ſubject to *Heraclius*, and form what is commonly called the kingdom of Georgia; as the four laſt, which are ſubject to *David*, form the kingdom or principality of Imeretia.

THIS whole country is ſo extremely beautiful, that ſome fanciful travellers have imagined they had here found the ſituation of the original garden of Eden. The hills are covered with foreſts of oak, aſh, beech, cheſnuts, walnuts, and elms, encircled with vines, growing perfectly wild, but producing vaſt quantities of grapes. From theſe is annually made as much wine as is neceſſary for the yearly consumption; the remainder are left to rot on the vines. Cotton grows ſpontaneouſly, as well as the fineſt European fruit-trees. Rice, wheat, millet, hemp, and flax, are raiſed on the plains, almoſt without culture. The valleys afford the fineſt paſturage in the world; the rivers are full of fiſh; the mountains abound in minerals, and the climate is delicious; ſo that nature appears to have laviſhed on this favoured country every production that can contribute to the happineſs of its inhabitants.

ON the other hand, the rivers of Georgia, being fed by mountain torrents, are at all ſeaſons either too rapid or too ſhallow

for

for the purpofes of navigation: the Black Sea, by which commerce and civilization might be introduced from Europe, has been 'till very lately in the exclufive poffeffion of the Turks: the trade of Georgia by land is greatly obftructed by the high mountains of Caucafus; and this obftacle is ftill increafed by the fwarms of predatory nations, by which thofe mountains are inhabited.

It is faid, that in the 15th century, a king of Georgia divided among his five fons the provinces of Carduel and Caket, Imeretia, Mingrelia, Guriel, and Abkhafia. Thefe petty princes were too jealous to unite for their common defence, and too weak fingly to refift a foreign enemy, or even to check the encroachments of their great vaffals, who foon became independent. By forming a party among thefe nobles, the Turks gradually gained poffeffion of all the weftern provinces, while the Perfians occupied the governments of Carduel and Caket. Since that period the many unfuccefsful attempts of the Georgians to recover their liberty, have repeatedly produced the devaftation of their country. *Abbas* the Great is faid to have carried off in one expedition from the provinces of Carduel and Caket no lefs than eighty thoufand families, a number which, probably, exceeds the whole actual population of thofe provinces. The moft horrible cruelties were again exercifed on the unhappy people, at the beginning of the prefent century, by the mercilefs *Nadir;* but thefe were trifling evils, compared with thofe arifing

from.

from the internal diffentions of the great barons. This numerous body of men, idle, arrogant, and ferocious, poffeffed of an
unlimited power over the lives and properties of their vaffals,
having no employment but that of arms, and no hopes of ag-
grandizing themfelves but by the plunder of their rivals, were
conftantly in a ftate of warfare; and as their fuccefs was various, and the peafants of the vanquifhed were conftantly carried
off and fold to the Turks or Perfians, every expedition increafed
the depopulation of the country. At length they invited the
neighbouring mountaineers, by the hopes of plunder, to take
part in their quarrels; and thefe dangerous allies, becoming acquainted with the country, and being fpectators of the weaknefs
of its inhabitants, foon completed its defolation. A few fqualid
wretches, half naked, half ftarved, and driven to defpair by the
mercilefs exactions of their landlords, are thinly difperfed over
the moft beautiful provinces of Georgia. The revolutions of
Perfia, and the weaknefs of the Turks, have indeed enabled the
princes of the country to recover their independence; but the
fmallnefs of their revenue has hitherto difabled them from re-
preffing effectually the tyranny of the nobles, and relieving the
burthens of the peafants.

The capital of Georgia, and place of refidence of prince
Heraclius, is Tifflis, called by the inhabitants Tbilis-Cabar
(warm town) from the warm baths in its neighbourhood. It
was founded, as appears by an old infcription in the citadel, by a

certain

certain prince *Lievang*, in the year 1063. Though its circum-
ference does not exceed two Englifh miles, it contains twenty
thoufand inhabitants, of which more than half are Armenians:
the remainder are principally Georgians, with fome Tartars.
It has twenty Armenian, and fifteen Greek churches, and three
Metfheds. The ftreets feldom exceed feven feet in breadth, and
fome are fo narrow as fcarcely to allow a paffage for a man on
horfeback: they are confequently very filthy. The houfes have
flat roofs, on which the women occafionally walk in fine weather:
they are neatly built, the walls of the rooms are wainfcotted, and
the floors fpread with carpets. At Tifflis there is a foundery, at
which are caft a few cannon, mortars, and balls, all of which
are very inferior to thofe of the Turks. The gunpowder made
here is very good. The Armenians have likewife eftablifhed in
this town all the manufactures carried on by their countrymen in
Perfia; the moft flourifhing is that of printed linens. The
common coins of Georgia are the abaffes, of about fifteen-pence
value, and a fmall copper coin, ftamped at the mint at Tifflis.
Befides thefe, a large quantity of gold and filver money is brought
into the country from Perfia and Turkey, in exchange for honey,
butter, cattle, and blue linens.

THE fubjects of *Heraclius* are eftimated at about fixty thoufand families; but this, notwithftanding the prefent defolated
ftate of the country, is probably an under valuation. The peafants belonging to the queen, and thofe of the patriarch, pay no

tax

tax to the prince, and therefore do not appear on the books of the revenue officers. Many fimilar exemptions have likewife been granted by the prince to his fons-in-law, and his favourites. Befides, as the impoft on the peafants is not a poll-tax, but a tax on hearths, the inhabitants of a village, on the approach of the collectors, frequently carry the furniture of feveral huts into one, and deftroy the remainder, which are afterwards very eafily replaced. It is probable, therefore, that the population of Georgia does not fall fhort of three hundred and fifty thoufand fouls.

THE revenues of this country may be eftimated at about 150,000 roubles, or 26,250l. They confift of, 1. the cuftoms, farmed at 1750l.—2. Rent paid by the farmers of the mint at Tifflis 1750l.—3. The tribute paid by the Khans of Erivan and Ganfha, 7000l.—and 4. The hearth money levied on the peafants, amounting to 15,750l.

THE government of Georgia is defpotic, but, were it not for the affiftance of the Ruffian troops, the prince would be frequently unable to carry his decrees into execution. The punifhments in criminal cafes are fhockingly cruel; fortunately they are not frequent, becaufe it is feldom difficult to efcape into fome of the neighbouring countries, and becaufe the prince is more enriched by confifcating the property of the criminal, than by putting him to torture. Judicial combats are confidered as the
privilege

privilege of nobility, and take place when the cause is extremely intricate, or when the power and interest of two claimants are so equal, that neither can force a decision of the court in his favour. This mode of trial is called an appeal to the judgment of God.

THE dress of the Georgians nearly resembles that of the Cosaks ; but men of rank frequently wear the habit of Persia. They usually dye their hair, beards, and nails with red. The Georgian women employ the same colour to stain the palms of their hands. On their heads they wear a cap or fillet, under which their black hair falls on their forehead : behind, it is braided into several tresses. Their eye-brows are painted with black, in such a manner as to form one intire line, and their faces are perfectly coated with white and red. Their robe is open to the girdle, so that they are reduced to conceal the breasts with their hands. Their air and manner are extremely voluptuous. Being generally educated in convents, they can all read and write ; a qualification which is very unusual among the men, even of the highest rank. Girls are betrothed as soon as possible, often at three or four years of age. In the streets the women of rank are always veiled, and then it is indecent in any man to accost them. It is likewise uncivil in conversation to enquire after the wives of any of the company. These, however, are not ancient customs, but are a consequence of the violences committed by the Persians, under Shach *Nadir*

TRA-

TRAVELLERS accuse the Georgians of drunkenness, superstition, cruelty, sloth, avarice, and cowardice; vices which are every where common to slaves and tyrants, and are by no means peculiar to the natives of this country. The descendants of the colonists, carried off by Shach *Abbas*, and settled at Peria, near Ispahan, and in Masanderan, have changed their character with their government; and the Georgian troops, employed in Persia against the Affghans, were advantageously distinguished by their docility, their discipline, and their courage.

THE other inhabitants of Georgia are Tartars, Ossi, and Armenians, called in the Georgian language Somakhi. These last are found all over Georgia, sometimes mixed with the natives, and sometimes in villages of their own. They speak among themselves their own language, but all understand and can talk the Georgian. Their religion is partly the Armenian, and partly the Roman Catholic. They are the most oppressed of the inhabitants, but are still distinguished by that instinctive industry which every where characterizes the nation.

BESIDES these, there are in Georgia confiderable numbers of Jews, called, in the language of the country, Uria.* Some have

villages

---

* According to *Gaerber*, there are numbers of Jews scattered over the provinces of Shirvan and Dagheftan; and he says, that they subfift principally by agriculture and raifing cattle,

villages of their own, and others are mixed with the Georgian, Armenian, and Tartar inhabitants, but never with the Offi. They pay a fmall tribute above that of the natives.

M. *Guldenflaedt* was permitted to make fome extracts from a manufcript chronicle in the Georgian language, compiled by order of *Vachtang*, late prince of Georgia, from the archives preferved in the monafteries of Gelati, near Cutais, and of Zcheta,. near Tifflis. This fingular hiftory ftates that

"In the year of the world 1792, there dwelt in a fortrefs, on mount Ararat, a man, of the name of *Targamos*. He lived fix hundred years, and was the father of eight fons : 1. *Aos*, from whom are defcended the Armenians. 2. *Kartelos*, from whom came the Kartuelta (Georgians). 3. *Baidos*, anceftor of the people of Raanta (Shirvan). 4. *Moakan*, from whom are defcended the Mokavnelta (people of Erivan). 5. *Lekas*, anceftor of the Lecta (Lefguis). 6. *Eros*, father of the Migrella (Mingrelians). 7. *Kaukas*, of the Kaukafianta (Caucafians). And 8. *Egros*, father of the Imeretians and Caketians.

"Of thefe fons the moft diftinguifhed was *Kartelos*. He had four fons, all of whom became *Mépé* (fovereigns). 1. *Obfe-*

rokos,

cattle, very few of them being employed in trade. He adds, that they are a very ancient colony : their Rabbins pretend that their forefathers were driven from Jerufalem into Media by the Muful *Padifhah*, or king of Niniveh.

rokos, who reigned over the country of Thafifkari, extending to the Black Sea (Imeretia and Mingrelia). 2. *Dſhavakhos,* who poſſeſſed the country of Parvanidkhon, as far as the Mtkuari (Kur) river. This ſeems to mean the diſtrict of Trianeti. 3. *Uplos,* king of the country from the river Aragui to the region of Thafifkari (the preſent province of Carduel). 4. *Charſarti,* who reigned over the country from Derbent to the Aragui.

" *Alexander Makedonaeli* (the Macedonian) came from Stioletti (the north) to Kartweli. At that time iniquity was at the higheſt pitch, and men committed uncleanneſs with their ſiſters, and even with cattle. *Alexander* came firſt before Chartis, and after-wards took ſucceſſively the cities of Odſrekal, Tſharochi, Up-lifziche, a very great city, Sarkine, Samſhilde, Zcheta, Urbniſi, Zichedidi, Aſpaulani, inhabited by Jews, Ruſtawi, Daldoziche, Btkurefziche, and all the cities of Caket. He left garriſons in all theſe cities, and eſtabliſhed himſelf at Zcheta, from whence he marched to Naſtakiſi, on the river Kſani. In Sarkinetti all perſons above 15 years of age were put to death.

" FROM the building of Rome, which happened 3233 years after *Adam,* to the days of *Merian,* there reigned in Georgia twenty-two *Mépés,* or ſovereigns (whoſe names are mentioned in the chronicle) ; and in the reign of *Merian,* in the year 338 after Chriſt, the female ſaint, *Nino,* together with the holy ſiſter, *Sidonia,* and the holy man, *Abrata,* arrived in this country, and

eſtabliſhed

eftablifhed the Chriftian religion."—After this follows a long catalogue of the fovereigns of Georgia, brought down to the prefent time ; but the foregoing extract will probably be fufficient to fatisfy the reader's curiofity.

THE capital of Imeretia, and place of refidence of prince *David*, is Cutais. The remains of its cathedral feem to prove that it was once a confiderable town, but at prefent it fcarcely deferves the name of a village. *Solomon*, father of the prefent prince, very wifely ordered the walls and the citadel to be deftroyed, obferving, that the rocks of Caucafus were the only fortifications which were capable of being defended by.an undifciplined army of fix thoufand men, unprovided with artillery.

THE inhabitants of Imeretia, eftimated at about twenty thoufand families, are not collected into towns or villages, but fcattered over the country in fmall hamlets. They are lefs mixed with foreigners, and handfomer than the other Georgians. They are likewife bolder, and more induftrious : they fend yearly confiderable quantities of wine to the neighbouring parts of Georgia, in leathern bags, carried by horfes : but they are without manufactures, very poor and miferable, and cruelly oppreffed by their vexatious landlords.

THE ordinary revenues of Imeretia, like thofe of Georgia, arife from a contribution of the peafants in wine, grain, and cattle,

·tle, and from the tribute of the neighbouring princes. Among the extraordinary fources of revenue, confifcations have a confiderable fhare; but as all this is by no means fufficient for the fubfiftence of the prince, he ufually travels from houfe to houfe, living on his vaffals, and never changing his quarters till he has confumed every thing eatable. It will of courfe be underftood, that the court of Imeretia is not remarkable for fplendour, nor the prince's table very fumptuoufly ferved. His ufual fare confifts of *gom* (a fpecies of millet, ground, and boiled into a pafte) a piece of roafted meat, and fome preffed caviar; thefe he eats with his fingers; forks and fpoons being unknown in Imeretia. At table he is frequently employed in judging caufes, which he decides at his difcretion, there being no law in his dominions but his own will.* His new ordinances are publifhed to the people on Fridays, which are the market days, by a crier, who gets up into a tree, and from thence iffues the proclamation.

THE Imeretians are of the Greek religion. Their Catholicos, or patriarch, is generally of the royal family, and can feldom read

---

* Judicial combats are in ufe in Imeretia and Mingrelia as well as in the reft of Georgia; but they are confined to the nobles. The trial by water ordeal is likewife fometimes practifed: but in civil cafes the Mingrelians have adopted a very rational kind of fubftitute for the common courts of juftice. Each party chufes a judge, and the two judges chufe one fpeaker. To him the plaintiff expofes his pretenfions, and then retires. The fpeaker then calls for the defendant, to whom he communicates the claim of his adverfary, and receives his anfwer. When the two parties have nothing more to fay, the two judges give their decifion.

read or write; and the inferior clergy are not better inftructed. Their churches are wretched buildings, fcarcely to be diftinguifhed from common cottages, but from a paper crofs over the principal door, and fome paintings of the Virgin and the faints.

The Dadian, or prince of Mingrelia and Guriel, though poffeffed of a country far more confiderable than Imeretia, is tributary to prince *David*, who is, therefore, a very formidable neighbour to the Turks of Achalziché. He is, however, very much fettered in his operations by the difobedience of his numerous barons, who, like thofe of Georgia and Mingrelia, have power of life and-death over their vaffals.

I   SPECIMEN

SPECIMEN

OF THE

CAUCASIAN LANGUAGES.

ABKHAS LANGUAGE.

	Altikefek Dialect.	*Cuban Dialect.*
God	Antſha	Antſha
Father	Oorak	Yaba
Mother	Anſhohk	Yan·
Son	Spau	Ippa
Daughter	Efa	Efa
Brother	Aſhey	Chee
Sifter	Ahkſhey	Khſha
Hufband	Skodza	Lkhadza
Wife	Stevſva	Pkhoos
Girl	Hyſha	Pkhoofpa
Boy	Spau	Arps
Child	Sitſkhoon	Tſhkoo-oon
Man	Goo	Agoo
People	Keet	Keet
Head	Yekka	Aka
Face	Eetſuymuyee	Etſuymuyee
Nofe	Pintſa	Pintſa
Eye	La	Oolla
Ear	Loomba	Limha
Forehead	Kapchk	Oolla
Hair	Leebray	Ijakay
Mouth	Eetcha.	Etcha

Teeth

ABKHAS LANGUAGE.

	Altikefck Dialect.	Cuban Dialect.
Teeth	Peets	Peets
Tongue	Eeps	Ibs
Beard	Jaikay	Ijakay
Neck	Yookda	Akda
Shoulder	Ecfhghvaka	Ecfhghva
Hand	Innappay	Impay
Fingers	Matfha	Mafhkhaba
Nails	Napkhay	Mamkhimnfa
Foot	Jappay	Shappay
Knee	Jamkhadedeerka	Keeka
Skin	Ectfha	Itfhayifh
Flefh	Jee	Jee
Bone	Bogo	Chont
Blood	Sha	Sha
Heart	Goo	Goo
Milk	Khfhay	Khfay
Sleep	Chkha	Deetcha
Love	Bjeddelgooee	
Pain	Eefafhkee	Afgheehkvee
Life	Echkee	Debgaoo
Death	Deefhee	Deefhta
Cold	Tkhta	Ehkta
Sun	Marah	Marah
Moon	Muys, Mazia	Mezzeh
Star	Aets, Bagooa	Yafs
Rain	Okvee	Kooah
Lightning	Attfey	Eematfoozvaee
Snow	Zeh	Zeh
Ice	Ttfafhch	Ttfafh
Day	Meeftchch	Meefh
Night	Bakah, Bakla	Bak
Evening	Koolpezy	

Summer

ABKHAS LANGUAGE.

	Altikefek Dialect.		*Cuban Dialect.*
Summer	Pkhneh		Apkh
Spring	Hapneh		Apna
Autumn	Bjayga		Atfneh
Winter	Gheen		Gheen
Year	Sheekoo, Skoofkeek	;	Skzeek
Earth	Atoola, Ttfoola	. .	Toola
Water	Dzeh, Seerreh . . .		Agoo
River	Zeddoo		Dzeddoo
Sand	Pfhahka		Pfhahka
Clay	Khantfy		Noofh
Mountain	Booko, Doo . . .		Boohk
Fire	Mtfch, Meetfa . . .		Meetfa
Heat	Pkha		Pkhaoo
Stone	Hak		Haook
Gold	Pkheh		Pkhee
Silver	Reefna		Reefna
Salt	Jeeka		Jeeka
Grafs	Ttfooa		Pfha
Tree	Ttflah		Ttflah

CIRCASSIAN

CIRCASSIAN of the CABARDAS.

God . . .	Tka, T-ha
Heaven . . .	Voo afay
Father . . .	Yada
Mother . .	Yana, Sana
Son . . .	Ko, Kookva
Daughter . .	Pkhoo
Brother . .	Stchay, Stchee
Sifter . . .	Cheepkhoo, Choopkh
Hufband . .	Tlay, Tlyce
Wife . . .	Fees, Eefyiz
Girl . . .	Hazebs, Pkhegebs
Boy . . .	Shaya, Chvalay
Child . . .	Zfhadla, Goo
Man . . .	Tfoog
People . .	Jeelay, Kookhfhel, Tfoogkher
Head . . .	Tfh-ha
Face . . .	Nap, Napa
Nofe . . .	Pay, Pa, Ja
Noftril . .	Pahk, P-ha
Eye . . .	Nay, Nejay
Eye-brows .	Nabtfa
Eye-lafhes .	Nekkepkh, Nejgoots
Ear . . .	T-hakooma
Forehead . .	Nafha
Hair . .	Sh-hats, Tfhkhaats
Cheeks . .	Takiaja, Takiaghay
Mouth . .	Jay, Dja
Throat . .	Tamak
Teeth . .	Dzay, Dza
Tongue . .	Bzaygoo, Bzek
Beard . .	Jakay
Neck . .	Pfhay
Shoulder . .	Damafha
Elbow . .	Zuytkha, Afarakka

Hand

CIRCASSIAN of the CABARDAS.

Hand	Ah
Fingers	Abkhuombay
Nails	Abjana
Belly	Nuyba, Negbay
Back	Cheefay, Chib
Foot	T-h-le, Skhlako
Knee	T-h-lagajay, Tlagoja, Tlegvadjay
Skin	Fa
Flefh	Lay, L-lay
Bone	Koobj-ha
Blood	T-hlay, Lay
Heart	Goo
Milk	Shay, Shchay
Hearing	Zekhekheen
Sight	Lagoon, Sofliaoo
Tafte	Afaoofa, Aiapf
Smelling	Immerpchanfh, Sfo-oo
Feeling	Teyabomupchitch, Sloteray
Voice	Mak
Name	Eetfa
Cry	Gooamak, mak
Noife	Pfmak, Kooa
Clamour	Khadaga, Pahka
Word	Jeezo-eo, Jjeepanner
Sleep	Jeay, Gheay, Jeateoo
Love	Chafla, Aitluiagoo
Pain	Ooz, Maooz
Toil	Kooghyakhan, Gooch
Work	Loja, Ohkwichen
Force	Gocha, Gvadj
Power	Dzlek, Gooacha
Authority	Pfhcego, Khveet
Marriage	Neekahk, Goofhaa
Life	Pfo-oogo

Stature

CIRCASSIAN of the CABARDAS.

Stature . .	Khekhon, Dſhekhon
Spirit . .	Bahkkha, Poofs
Death .	Khkhada, Tlen
Cold .	Shahay, Chyah
Circle .	Koorahay
Globe .	Tope, Khorlay
Sun . . .	Digga, Dweega, Ddaga
Moon . ..	Maza, Mazay
Star . . .	Bago, Bagwo, Yachah
Ray . .	Nehk, Deegapaayez
Wind . . .	Gjee
Whirlwind .	Jeebzag, Wojuykooee
Storm . . .	Joobahay
Rain . . .	Ooaſhkh, Oochkſh, Bohejkh
Hail . . .	Ooaſa, Bwoohof
Lightning .	Khobſkay, Kopk
Snow . . .	Wafs, Wefs, Bwooefs
Ice . . .	Mwil, Mel, Meel
Day . .	Atchnoo, Mahko, Makhooa
Night .	Jet, Gjegſh
Morning .	Nakhooſh, Pſhadeechas
Evening . .	Pſheghaſhga, Pſhabbay
Summer . .	Gamakva, Gammakho, Eetleſskol
Spring . . .	Gatkh
Autumn . .	Zeenay
Winter . . .	Jeemakva
Year . . .	Eetlias
Time . . .	Yoogoh, Paaſley
Earth . . .	Ch, Chwee
Water . . .	Sirray
Sea . . .	Khaoo
River . .	Pſookho, Pſooſhkvo
Waves . .	Pewer, Toolkoon
Sand . .	Pſhahko, Pſhahkooa Pſhahkaoo

Clay

CIRCASSIAN of the CABARDAS.

Clay . .	Yatta
Dust . . .	Sava, Sappa
Dirt . .	Yatta
Mountain .	Kooshkha, Bghee
Coast . .	Oofa, Nuyghay
Hill . . .	Ashkha, Tloolghay
Valley .	Tchlashka, Kooa
Air . . .	Obshook
Vapour . .	Antkhoplshkashoo, Bakha
Fire . . .	Maffa, Maafa
Heat . . .	Jegoopl, Khoolba, Khvaba
Depth . .	Koo, Eckooag
Height . .	Khlaghy, Aootlejag
Breadth . .	Boohk, Eeboogag
Length . . .	Kehkag, Eekehkahk
Hole . . .	Gooana, Wana
Pit . . .	Masha, Mashay
Ditch . . .	Cheetoga, Tuycha
Stone . . .	Muyvoa, Muyvwy
Gold . .	Duyshay, Deeshah
Silver . . .	Djeen, Duyjeen
Salt . . .	Shoog, Shoogoog, Choog
Miracle . .	Chagho
Forest . . .	Mez, Miez
Grass . .	Oots, Oods
Tree . .	Jeeg, Pkha
Pole . . .	Bjohk, Pjohg
Verdure . .	Oots, Shkhondahcha

OSETIAN

OSETIAN LANGUAGE.

	Dialect of Oseti.	Dialect of Dugor.
God	Tfa-oo	Khoo-tfa-oo
Heaven	Arv . . .	Arv
Father	Feed . . .	Feeday
Mother	Emmad, Mad . .	Madai
Son	Feert, Lapoo .	Foort
Daughter	Kyfgui . .	Kyfgui
Brother	Arvadey, Ervod .	Arvod
Sifter	Kho, Ekhoo . .	Khorra
Hufband	Moee, Emmoee .	Moeenay
Wife	Oos . . .	Oaffa
Girl	Kyfgay, Ekhootak .	Kyfgay
Boy	Lapoo . .	Lokkon
Child	Sevellom, Lapoo .	Bidjiaoo
Man	Leg, Lahk . . .	Leg
People	Adamta . . .	Adamta
Head	Zer, Effar . . .	Zer
Face	Etchafkom, Tfefkom .	Etchafkom
Nofe	Findj, Fens . . .	Finds
Noftril	Thinzakhonkhetty .	Efinjykhoonk
Eye	Tfvettay, Cheft, Chafht .	Tfeftay
Eye-brow	Tfeftaythaltay, Erfeet .	Erfeet
Eye-lafhes	Khaltay, Erkta . . .	
Ear	Khoos, Oos, Koos . .	Gos
Forehead	Yennihk, Nihk, Ennahk .	Ternihk
Hair	Dzeekoo, Zibkoo, Effarkhoon	Djeckko
Cheeks	Rooftay, Evadoohkta . .	Rooftay
Mouth	Tfoog, Zuyhk, Tfhuyhk .	Tfoog
Throat	Cure	Ekkoor
Teeth	Dandak	Dendak
Tongue	Afzagkay, Vzag, Abzag .	Afzaghay
Beard	Reehky, Botfoo, Bodjo .	Rehkay
Neck	Aftfeg, Efchak . . .	Aftfeg

K   Shoulder

OSETIAN LANGUAGE

	Ofeti.	*Dugor.*
Shoulder	Tfong, Evchak	Tfong
Elbow	Rambwin, Orak	
Hand	Kohk, Koohk	Koohk
Fingers	Koohkalhk, Koohktay, Nahkta	Angoolfay
Nails	Naehk, Nihktay, Yalg	Nachk
Belly	Goobynn	
Back	Feffontay, Efkaldan	
Foot	Kahk	Kahk
Knee	Oorag, Orak	Waragay
Skin	Tfarn, Srak, Cardj	Tfarn
Flefh	Fid, Thid	Fid
Bone	Afteg, Eeftahk	Afteg
Blood	Artendy, Toog	Too-oog
Heart	Zarda	Serd, Serdey
Milk	Ahkfuyr, Ihkfuyr	Ahkfheer
Hearing	Koofen, Fekkoofta	
Sight	Tfyunen, Ooney	
Tafte	Adgheen	
Smelling	Smag, Shmak	
Feeling	Anbaren, Archagfta	
Voice	Kalas, Djeerd	
Name	Nom	
Cry	Ekkar, Keery	
Noife	Calebah	
Clamour	Kaoon	
Word	Djeerd, Zuyrd	
Sleep	Khoozeg, Khoos	Khooffek
Love	Warayen, Barjey	
Pain	Ruynkeen Reece	Rooh
Toil	Keyamat, Narv	
Work	Kiooft, Koottak	
Force	Tuyhk, Ezcer	

Power

OSETIAN LANGUAGE.

	Ofeti.	*Dugor.*
Power	Tkheen, Teekkeen . .	
Authority	Ebboon, Khorfag . .	
Marriage	Keenzavfeg, Keengiakzav .	
Life	Tfernebon, Gas . .	Tferroon
Stature	Rez, Sevfardee . .	
Spirit	Smag, Shmak ، .	
Death	Malat, Mard . .	Molluyn, Mard
Cold	Bazal, Eehkan . .	Ekhon
Circle	Khahk, Tymbull . .	
Globe	Tuynbuyn ، . .	
Sun	Khoor	Khor
Moon	Meyee, Ma-yee ، .	Ma-yeh
Star	Stalat, Stella, Staleh . .	Stalooteh
Ray	Khooreten, Khoort . .	
Wind	Duymee, Bahad . .	
Whirl- } wind }	Duymghy, Teembal . .	
Storm	Abzyoorybwoonty, Bodkanny	
Rain	Bar, Wahran . . .	Kabda
Hail	Eehk . ، .	
Lightning	Bacheelaekar, Perfta, Àrbateef	Artey
Snow	Meed . . .	Meddy
Ice	Eehk, Yeehk ، . .	Yehk
Day	Bon . . .	Bon
Night	Ahkfaf, Ahkfev ، .	Ahkfava
Morning	Raheefo, Raheefoon . ،	
Evening	Eezar, Zer, Zar . .	
Summer	Serd, Faffek . ، .	Sardey
Spring	Walzak . . .	Waldzak
Autumn	Aragfaffek . .	Ragfaffek
Winter	Zoomok . . .	Zoomak
Year	Afadjoo, Az, Ans, Yafadfh .	Ans
Time	Ragooo . . .	
Earth	Zahk, Cheegheet . .	Cheegheet

Water

OSETIAN LANGUAGE.

	Oſeti.	*Dugor.*
Water	Don	Don
Sea	Foord	
River	Don	Don·
Waves	Farſalak	
Sand	Amees	Ajmieſſa
Clay	Keer, Cheef	Cheegheet
Duſt	Ruyk, Ruyg	
Dirt	Tſuyf, Cheef	
Mountain	Khohk	Khong
Coaſt	Buyl, Donabuyl	
Hill	Tuypuyr, Arak	
Valley	Thetten-beſtey, Ardoos	
Air	Roohks	
Vapour	Tef, Tabd	
Fire	Art, Zuyng	Djeeng
Heat	Tſahkar, Sinkytapar	Antef
Depth	Arf	
Height	Ooleyaoo, Arzond	
Breadth	Theten, Korg	
Length	Darhk	
Hole	Khonka, Khoonk	
Pit	Oovaruym, Djeek	
Ditch	Ooverm, Darkhahkt	
Stone	Door	Attoor, Dor
Gold	Suyzgary, Soohkzerreen	Zoohkzareeny
Silver	Abzyſs, Abzyſt	Agooyeſta, Ajoſheſta
Salt	Sahk, Chahk	Tſankheh
Miracle	Deeſag	
Foreſt	Kad	
Graſs	Kuyrdey, Khos	Khoaſſa
Tree	Ballas, Pallas, Soog	Balahaſſey, Jog
Pole	Meehk, Seertmeehk	
Verdure	Tſahk, Kardakhos	

LANGUAGE

LANGUAGE of the KISTI.

	Dialect of Tchetchens.	*Dialect of the Ingoushi.*
God	D-yaly	D-yala
Heaven	Stuygley	Seeghelich
Father	Da	Da
Mother	Naana	Nana
Son	Ya	Ya
Daughter	Yohay	Yoogheek
Brother	Vafhay, Vooafha	Vafha
Sifter	Efhau, Ghefha	Efha
Hufband	Maar, Kuanahk	Maar
Wife	Eeftyoo, Sknellyn	Zyelk, Syee
Girl	Yohay, Yoau	Yoogheek
Boy	Bayar	Bayiree
Child	Beeyer, Bayar	Beeyer
Man	Steg	Stag, Sek
People	Naahk, Dookanahk	Naahk
Head	Korto, Kartay	Kortay, Kwartay
Face	Yookhay, Yohk	Yoohkmerinn
Nofe	Maray	Meerha, Merj
Noftril	Maray-oorgefh	Mertchoorgeefh
Eye	Baireek, Bareek	Berg, Pairg
Eye-brow	Satfgamefh	Teggeelam
Eye-lafh	Barghen-neegheen	Bergentchooifh
Ear	Lerrik	Lerk
Forehead	Hajay, Khiaeezay	Hadjay, Kheejay
Hair	Kajorefh, Chooa	Befhkennifh, Koodj
Cheeks	Befny	Beckelnghill
Mouth	Daghay, Baghay	Yeeft, Bagga
Throat	Lyak	Kyarmuyky
Teeth	Tferghyfh, Tferrefh	Tferghyt
Tongue	Mot, Moot	Mottay
Beard	Maj, Miaj, Miav	Mekkafh, Chingh
Neck	Bartaday, Yany	Faart, Ferto

Shoulder

LANGUAGE of the KISTI.

	Dialect of Tchetchens.	*Dialect of the Ingoushi.*
Shoulder	Pkhanaret	Bailam
Elbow	Gwaala	Gwalla
Hand	Kooyk, Kooky . .	Koolg, Koolkoo
Fingers	Paleek, Telgefh . .	Palk, Pelgeefh
Nails	Maray, Maagaren .	Maray, Merghin
Belly	Gahay . .	Gueeky, Bueeky
Back	Bookg . . .	Booko
Foot	Kohk, Kok . .	Kog
Knee	Gooala . .	Gooa, Varoo
Skin	Kaka, Tfhkoora .	Kaka, Tfooalka
Flefh	Gheefhik, Beeleekly .	Deehlk
Bone	Daahkket, Deeyahk .	Tehkk
Blood	T-tfee, Tfee . ..	T-tfee
Heart	Dook .	Dog
Milk	Shyrrey, Shoorey .	Shyrrey, Shooro
Hearing	Khazar . .	Kheddees
Sight	Deher . .	Goofhuan
Tafte	Leeair . .	Merfeenday
Smelling	Kh-haajoo . .	Merdj
Feeling	Laatfer .	Kuydeedeas
Voice	Eefh . .	Tfaga
Name	Deen . .	Tfey
Cry	Anekkeen .	Garee
Noife	Sellay . .	Gargahts-tfoo
Clamour	Bonkheelen .	Belkkery, Deermas
Word	Doofh . .	Doofh
Sleep	Gan .	Naap, Bajee
Love	Veeezay, Kooezay .	Bedzetfuan
Pain	Oon . .	Mogats, Mogots
Toil	Doo-ookher .	Kadakhoonzoo
Work	Boolhk .	Booelhk
Force	Neetfkey .	Neets

Power

LANGUAGE of the KISTI.

	Dialect of Tchetchens.	*Dialect of the Ingoushi.*
Power	Dookatfaagoon	Nad, Nats
Authority	Makokheelar	Seenatfa
Marriage	Makhar-beeliar	Noofkoldarembafo
Life	Kkhan	Dentfek, Betaloveh
Stature	Lakadaalar, Lakeedaar	Kh-khah
Spirit	Efch, Sfay	Eh
Death	Balar	Belleen, Layghee
Cold	Sheeyeleen	Sheely, Shel
Circle	Gooe	Goohoo
Globe	Goorghendeh	Goo-orghee
Sun	Malyk	Malyk
Moon	Boofh	Bute, Booto
Star	Syed, Seeyeddeh	Zetta, Zuta
Ray	Tkhahk	Merkhendenerj
Wind	Mohk	Moohk
Whirlwind	Yahatchoony	Foo-o
Storm	Ourefhtekeen	Eeatcheeghch
Rain	Dogoo, Dougoo, Dagoo	Dohoh
Hail	Kwaroo	Shwyfheeheh
Lightning	Steeglyaikey, Nooryftegan	Tazehgo, Dekooka
Snow	Looa	La, Loho
Ice	Kheelen	Sha, Shebelek
Day	Deeyeeny, Deeyeenchk	Den, Deh
Night	Booffoo	Boozee, Buyta, Booceffay
Morning	Yarroo, Oorioo	Soorey
Evening	Sarrahk, Sarehk	Seyeery
Summer	Baftee	Baftee, Shu
Spring		Goora
Autumn		Ahkk
Winter		Aee
Year	Shooa	Tfafhoo, Tiafhwoh
Time	Laan	Tagandehkeendeday
Earth	Lettchk, Latta	Liate, Lette

3

Water

LANGUAGE OF THE KISTI.

	Dialect of Tchetchens.	*Dialect of the Ingoushi.*
Water	Khee	Khice
Sea	Khort	Foort
River	Malar	Dokankhee, Khice
Waves	Toolgoonet	Khiceftedete
Sand	Goom	Teih, Goom
Clay	Khat	Tapoor, Ker
Duft	Chen	Doma
Dirt	Keeleeyet	Khottey
Mountain	Lam	Lamartch, Beerd
Coaft	Eeyet	Shoo-oo
Hill	Eerakhooa	Bartfay
Valley	Bieeroo	Khozleroo
Air	Lekkeeyeh	Mogofhyee
Vapour	Koor	Egog
Fire	Tfeeyeh	T-tfeh, Tfuy
Heat	Yahookhen	Taoo, Yawehkey
Depth	Kargoon	Kargo
Height	Tkyeehk	Liakkay-khallay
Breadth	Latteh	Shoogra
Length	Dehehken	Deahkay
Hole	Ooreek	Yoorka
Pit	Tkhag	Lerma
Ditch	Ahk-ker	Booroog
Stone	Toolak	Kera
Gold	Betyee	Detaoo, Dehtoo
Silver	Detee	Detaoo, Detoo
Salt	Tookhee	Toohk
Miracle	Tamatabar	Tameeuyt
Foreft	Khioon	Khioon
Grafs	Boots	Boots, Yol
Tree	Khen	Kheh; Datcheck
Pole	Khaakoo	Doohkk
Verdure	Sengheleen	Seniee

LESGUIS LANGUAGE.

	Dialects of Antſboug,	Dſhar,	Chunſagh,	Dido.
God	Bedſhet .	Bedſhet .	Bedjet . .	Bedſhet
Heaven	Zob	Zob . .	Zob . .	Zoub
Father	Dayday .	Dayday .	Daddy .	Obeeo
Mother	Ebbel, Evel .	Evel .	Ebbel . .	Enneeyoo
Son	Timmeer .	Khimmeer .	Timmeer .	Takvee-ooſhee, Ooſhee
Daughter	Yaz .	Yas . .	Yaz . .	Kid
Brother	Yats .	Yats . .	Vaas . .	Gloocheſſeeo
Sister	Heeats .	Heeats . .	Yas .	Akkiyeſſio
Husband	Bikhintchy .	Jennelaoochee	Bikkhichy .	Tkeddioo
Wife	Choojo .	Jennelaoochaba	Choojoo .	Dya, Broo
Girl	Yaſſy .	Yaſſy . .	Yaſſy .	Kidd
Boy	Ooaſſa . .	Ooaſſa .	Vaas .	Ooſhy
Child	Teemeer .	Khimmeer .	Timmeer .	Takveeooſhee
Man	Bahartſh .	Bahartſhy .	Bahartſhy .	Checkvy
People	Emmeraoodjy	Jammahad .	Oſh, Adamal .	Oſh, Adam
Head	Betterr .	Bekkerr .	Betterr .	Tkeen
Face	Berkbal .	Berkbal . .	Berkbal .	
Nose	Khoomoohg .	Mooſhooſh .	Khomak .	Malee
Nostril		Kallee .		
Eye	Beayerr .	Beayerr, Bear	Beayerr .	Ozioorabbee
Eye-brow	Kroontſrool .	Kroontſrool .		
Eye-lashes	Berzoolas .	Berzoolas .	Berzoolas .	
Ear	Inn .	Ayinn .	Aenn .	Ahayaby
Forehead	Nodoh .	Noodoh .	Nodo .	Tlokva
Hair	Zab . .	Ras .	Zab .	Kody
Cheeks	Khoomeer .	Khoomeer .	Khoomeer .	
Mouth	Kaal, Kyal .	Kaal .	Kaal .	Hakoo
Throat	Seckair .	Seckair .	Sekkair .	
Teeth	Zeeby .	Zeeby .	Tſaby, Tſavy	Keetſoo
Tongue	Ma-ots .	Ma-ots .	Ma-ots .	Mets
Beard	Ma-ej .	Ma-ej .	Ma-ej .	Meſhholga
Neck	Gooboor .	Gaboor .	Gaboor .	Mitſh
Shoulder	Boohoon .	Getſh .	Geſh .	Hero
Elbow	Kayſhay .		Kayſhay .	
Hand	Kooer, Kver .	Kver .	Kver .	Retla

L

Fingers

LESGUIS LANGUAGE.

Dialects of Antſhoug,		Dſhar,	Chunſagh,	Dido.
Fingers	Nats . .	Gheeleeſh .	Gheelceſh, Keeſhal	Baſheebee
Nails	Maat . .	Maahk .	Matl . .	Motlooghy
Belly	Chchk .	Chchk .	Chchk .	
Back	Moohk .	Moohk .	Moohk .	
Foot	Pog .	Pog . .	Pog . .	Rorec
Knee	Nakoo .	Googa .	Nakoo .	Eknokoo
Skin	Khegg .	Kegg .	Tſoko . .	Beek
Fleſh	Han . .	Han . .	Han . .	Retl
Bone	Ratla . .	Reeka .	Radla .	Tloofa
Blood	Bee . .	Bee . .	Bee . .	A.
Heart	Rak . .	Rak .	Rak . .	Roko
Milk	Rahk . .	Rahk .	Rahk . .	Ghay
Hearing		Riabla .		
Sight		Beekhoola .		
Taſte		Konahla .		
Smelling		Miahkcholla		
Feeling		Kheella .		
Voice		Kharatl .		
Name		Tſarſheep .		
Cry		Kharatell .		
Noiſe		Debl . .		
Clamour		Eddoola .		
Word		Rayee .		
Sleep	Matlee	Matlo . .	Matlo .	
Love		Otlooloh .		
Pain		Oontee .		
Toil		Zahkmat .		
Work		Khialtee .		
Force		Koobat .		
Power		Bojee-booghy		
Authority		Seev-khaldee-doohk-ooghoo		
Marriage		Makkiareeton		
Life		Khleekhoog-heeſh		
Stature		Kliuana .		

Death

LESGUIS LANGUAGE.

Dialects of Antſhoug,		Dſhar,	Chunſagh,	Dido.
Death		Khana .		Haratch
Cold	Rohee .	Khooatchala	Rohee . .	Rohee
Circle		Akeever .		
Globe		Goorgheenaoo		
Sun	Baak .	Baak . .	Baak .	Book
Moon	Mo-ots, Motſh	Mo-ots .	Mo-ots .	Bootſee
Star	Tſoah .	Tſavee .	Tſoah .	Tſah
Ray		Bab, Bakoon		
Wind		Khooree .		
Whirlwind		Khiooree .		
Storm		Zob-abargoon		
Rain	Tſad .	Tſaat .	Tſad .	Kemma
Hail		Goro .		
Lightning	Pree . .	Pree, Peerree	Peer .	Maktl
Snow	Azoo . .	Azo . .	Arzoo .	Eeſſee
Ice	Riee . .	Tſooer, Tſer	Tſooer .	Berroo
Day	Ko . .	Ko . .	Djaka .	Djekkool
Night	Zoordo .	Khaſſey .	Zoordo .	Gheedod
Morning		Radaleeſa .		
Evening		Bakkareeta .		
Summer	Reeyee .	Reedal, Yooer-my	Reedal .	Semmeetl
Spring	Echktee .	Echktee .	Okhoſſa .	Atohk
Autumn	Khazeel .	Khazeel .	Khazab .	Imkho
Winter	Tyilleen .	Tyilleen .	Khazel .	Etlermo
Year	Zozo . .	Zozo . .	Taggett .	Tlebby
Time		Reehkboochoo		
Earth, Land	Ratl . .	Riatl . .	Ratl .	Cheddo
Water	Gtleem .	Khleem .	Gtleem .	Gtlee
Sea		Rahkiad .		
River	Or .	Or, Khiar .	Khor .	Eggoo
Waves		Bagaroola .		
Sand		Khoom .		
Clay	Chabbar .	Khiaſh, Chab-bar	Chabbar .	Cheddo
Duſt		Khioor .		
Dirt		Khiaſh . .		

Mountain

LESGUIS LANGUAGE.

Dialects of	Antſhoug,	Dſhar,	Chunſagh,	Dido.
Mountain	Mayerr .	Mayerr .	Tlooroo .	Tillad
Coaſt		Rayall .		
Hill		Mayerr .		
Valley		Kauley .		
Air		Koo-o .		
Vapour		Kooee . .		
Fire	Tſah .	Tſyah .	Tſah . .	Tſce
Heat	Khentee .	Kheenkhloo .	Khentee .	Khentee
Depth			Gvoarreeda .	
Height			Reechadaa .	
Breadth			Evva .	
Length			Khalagvada .	
Hole		.	Karat .	
Pit			Bakka .	
Ditch			Tattaool .	
Stone	Teb . .	Khetſoh . .	Eetſo .	Gool
Gold	Mezet .	Mezed .	Mezet .	Ookroo
Silver	Arats .	Arats .	Arats .	Meetſkheer
Salt	Tſam .	Tſam .	Tſyan .	Tſecyo
Miracle			Tamata .	
Foreſt			Tſool .	
Graſs			Tkherr .	
Tree			Tſogooet .	
Pole			Kazeck .	
Verdure			Yoorcheena- boogoo	

GEORGIAN

GEORGIAN LANGUAGE.

	Carduel Dialect.	*Imeretian.*	*Suaneti Dialect.*
God	Gmerty	Horomti	Gherbet
Heaven	Tfah	Tfafh	Tfah
Father	Mamma	Moona	Moo
Mother	Dedda	Deeda	Dee
Son	Shyilly	Skooa	Yezag
Daughter	Kaly	Ozoory	Zoonak
Brother	Tfmah	Djeema	Moohkbay
Sifter	Da	Datchkym	Datchoor
Hufband	Kmary	Komodjy	Chafh
Wife	Tfoly	Cheely	Aikhoo
Girl	Kally	Ozoory	Soorag
Boy	Bidjaoo	Bidjaoo	Tfhkynta
Child	Kmatfvilly, Tfvilly, Krmah	Bofhy	Bobfh
Man	Kadtfy	Kodfhy	Maray
People	Khalkhee, Erny, Catfuy	Margalee	Khvace-maray
Head	Tavee, Kavee	Doodee	Tkhoom
Face	Peeraffa, Sakhay, Peeris-fakhay	Peejeefhee	
Nofe	Tfkhveery	Tchkhin-dee	Yepkhna
Noftril	Nefto, Neftvy		
Eye	Twaly, Tvaly	Toly	Tay
Eyebrow	Tfarby		
Eyelafhes	Khaltay, Erkta		
Ear	Koory	Oodjy	Shdeem
Forehead	Shoobly	Kooa	Neekba
Hair	Tma	Toma	Patoo
Cheeks	Loka, Koba		
Mouth	Peeree	Pidjee	Peel
Throat	Kharkhanto, Tkelly		
Teeth	Kbeely, Gbeely	Keebeery	Shdik
Tongue	Aina	Neena	Nin
Beard	Tfverry, Tfverry	Preemooly	Waray
Neck	Kifferry, Kaily	Kifferry	Kinfhkh
Shoulder	Pkary, Mkhary	Khoodjy	Mekher
Elbow	Dakvy, Tfkrtah		

Hand

GEORGIAN LANGUAGE.

	Carduel Dialect.	Imeretian.	Suaneti Dialect.
Hand	Kehelly, Khelly	Kheh	Shee
Fingers	Teetee, Teetebbee, Titnee	Keetee	Pkhooyay
Nails	Fchinly, Pchkhelly, Prchkheclebby	Byrtekha	Tfkhah
Belly	Mootfelly		
Back	Zoorghy		
Foot	Fayghee, Paykhee, Pekky	Koochkhy	Cheefhkh
Knee	Mookly, Moohkly	Boorgooly	Gweyee
Skin	Tkhavee	Tkhebby	Kan
Flefh	Khortfy, Kartfy	Khortfy	Yekhoo
Bone	Tfwally, Tfzvally	Tfwally	Tjeego
Blood	Seefkhly	Seefkhelly	Yemmefk
Heart	Goolee	Gooree	Goo
Milk	Rtfch, Rdzay	Bjah	Eerdjeh
Hearing	Gogonebba, Safmenelee		
Sight	Kebvelaba, Kedva		
Tafte	Ghemovneba, Ghemo		
Smelling	Knofla, Knofeba		
Feeling	Shehkeba, Gankheelba, Goorzeenova		
Voice	Khmah		
Name	Sakhely		
Cry	Kveereely, Dfahkely		
Noife	Kakanee, Grgveenba, Tchkoobee		
Clamour	Teereleegodeva, Tkebba		
Word	Saubaree, Seetkhva		
Sleep	Dzeely, Seefmaree	Looree	Looree
Love	Seekvarooly, Ookvar	Worts	
Pain	Tkeeveely, Salmoba		
Toil	Gartcheelova, Shroma, Sardjelee		
Work	Moofhakova, Moofhaova		
Force	Tfzalee, Gonay		
Power	Dzalee, Gonch		
Authority	Cheelova, Chedleba, Khelmfteepaiba		
Marriage	Shayooglebba, Kortfeeneba		
Life	Tfuytfotfhkhley, Tfkhovraba		
Stature	Taneefegzdeelova, Tanee, Agzda, Hazda		

Spirit

GEORGIAN LANGUAGE.

	Carduel Dialect.	Imeretian.	Suaneti Dialect.
Spirit	Soolee		
Death	Sikvdeela, Stfchoolee		
Cold	Tfcetfych, Seetfkhch, Scetfceevch		
Circle	Mgoorgaly, Mergva-leatfre, Symgrgvleh		
Globe	Boorfhy, Mgoorbaly		
Sun	Mzeh	Bja	Mcej
Moon	Mtwary, Mtvary	Toota	Mij
Star	Mafkulavy, Varfeclavy	Mooroots	Antkvefk
Ray	Shoofhee, Skecevce, Sharavandee		
Wind	Nyahvee, Karee, Kwheeree		
Storm	Bookee, Brtfelgelba, Neeflee		
Rain	Tfuyma, Tfveema	Cheema	Ootchga
Hail	Setkva		
Lightning	Elva, Elvareba	Valy	Elvaee
Snow	Tovlee	Terree	Moos
Ice	Kinnooly, Keenoobly	Eence	Kvarem
Day	Dghch	Ga	Defhdwee
Night	Gam, Gamey	Zerry	Leket
Morning	Deela		
Evening	Sagamo, Mtfookhry		
Summer	Zapkhooly, Tfelnice		
Spring	Gazapooly		
Autumn	Shamodgoma		
Winter	Zamtary		
Year	Ttfeleetfadee	Tfanamatfana	Sahee
Time	Dro, Jamee		
Earth	Meetfa	Dechka	Gheem
Water	Tfkaly, Tfkhaly	Ttfkary	Veets
Sea	Zgvebby, Zgva		
River	Bdeenary, Mdeenary		Gangalits
Waves	Ghelva, Ghelvany		
Sand	Khoomy, Kveefha		
Clay	Teekhah, Talakhee		Gheem
Dust	Mftverry		Dirt

GEORGIAN LANGUAGE.

	Carduel Dialect.	Imeretian.	Suaneti Dialect.
Dirt	Lapce, Talakhce		
Mountain	Keeldeh, Mtah	Keerdey	Kodj
Coaft	Tfkleefnapeery, Napeera, Plato .		
Hill	Sevvee, Bortfvee . . .		
Valley	Vakeh, Baree, Velly . . .		
Ar	Atchry, Hahery		
aipour	Ortkly, Ortkhly . . .		
Fire	Tfetfkhlee · . .	Datfhkh-ley	Hemmck
Heat	Nakvertfkhaly . . .	Tbeela	
Depth	Seegrmcy		
Height	Seemagley		
Breadth	Seeganyerry		
Length	Seegrtfch, Seegfay . . .		
Hole	Nakvrety		
Pit	Ormo		
Ditch	Ruby, Tkhrebly . .		
Stone	Kva	Kooa	Kva
Gold	Okro	Mokro	Oker
Silver	Bertfkhlee . . .	Kvartch-khcely	Bertfkh-lch
Salt	Marecly	Joomy	Gheem
Miracle	Sakoorvely		
Foreft	Tkeh, Tkhch, Tenkch . .		
Grafs	Balakhce, Teeva . . .		
Tree	Tkhertkey, Khay . . .	Tkah	Tfkhekka
Pole	Palo, Margheely . . .		
Verdure	Mtfvaneely, Tfvanveely . . .		

F I N I S.

www.ingramcontent.com/pod-product-compliance
Lightning Source LLC
Chambersburg PA
CBHW021427090426
42742CB00009B/1290

* 9 7 8 3 7 4 4 7 5 7 4 3 0 *